CHINA'S ADVANCE IN LATIN AMERICA AND THE CARIBBEAN

JOINT HEARING

BEFORE THE

SUBCOMMITTEE ON THE WESTERN HEMISPHERE

AND THE

SUBCOMMITTEE ON ASIA AND THE PACIFIC

OF THE

COMMITTEE ON FOREIGN AFFAIRS HOUSE OF REPRESENTATIVES

ONE HUNDRED FOURTEENTH CONGRESS

FIRST SESSION

SEPTEMBER 10, 2015

Serial No. 114–95

Printed for the use of the Committee on Foreign Affairs

Available via the World Wide Web: http://www.foreignaffairs.house.gov/ or http://www.gpo.gov/fdsys/

U.S. GOVERNMENT PUBLISHING OFFICE

96–051PDF   WASHINGTON : 2015

For sale by the Superintendent of Documents, U.S. Government Publishing Office
Internet: bookstore.gpo.gov   Phone: toll free (866) 512–1800; DC area (202) 512–1800
Fax: (202) 512–2104   Mail: Stop IDCC, Washington, DC 20402–0001

COMMITTEE ON FOREIGN AFFAIRS

EDWARD R. ROYCE, California, *Chairman*

CHRISTOPHER H. SMITH, New Jersey
ILEANA ROS-LEHTINEN, Florida
DANA ROHRABACHER, California
STEVE CHABOT, Ohio
JOE WILSON, South Carolina
MICHAEL T. McCAUL, Texas
TED POE, Texas
MATT SALMON, Arizona
DARRELL E. ISSA, California
TOM MARINO, Pennsylvania
JEFF DUNCAN, South Carolina
MO BROOKS, Alabama
PAUL COOK, California
RANDY K. WEBER SR., Texas
SCOTT PERRY, Pennsylvania
RON DeSANTIS, Florida
MARK MEADOWS, North Carolina
TED S. YOHO, Florida
CURT CLAWSON, Florida
SCOTT DesJARLAIS, Tennessee
REID J. RIBBLE, Wisconsin
DAVID A. TROTT, Michigan
LEE M. ZELDIN, New York
DANIEL DONOVAN, New York

ELIOT L. ENGEL, New York
BRAD SHERMAN, California
GREGORY W. MEEKS, New York
ALBIO SIRES, New Jersey
GERALD E. CONNOLLY, Virginia
THEODORE E. DEUTCH, Florida
BRIAN HIGGINS, New York
KAREN BASS, California
WILLIAM KEATING, Massachusetts
DAVID CICILLINE, Rhode Island
ALAN GRAYSON, Florida
AMI BERA, California
ALAN S. LOWENTHAL, California
GRACE MENG, New York
LOIS FRANKEL, Florida
TULSI GABBARD, Hawaii
JOAQUIN CASTRO, Texas
ROBIN L. KELLY, Illinois
BRENDAN F. BOYLE, Pennsylvania

AMY PORTER, *Chief of Staff*   THOMAS SHEEHY, *Staff Director*
JASON STEINBAUM, *Democratic Staff Director*

CONTENTS

_____

CHINA'S ADVANCE IN LATIN AMERICA AND THE CARIBBEAN

THURSDAY, SEPTEMBER 10, 2015

House of Representatives,
Subcommittee on the Western Hemisphere and
Subcommittee on Asia and the Pacific,
Committee on Foreign Affairs,
Washington, DC.

The subcommittees met, pursuant to notice, at 2:22 p.m., in room 2172, Rayburn House Office Building, Hon. Jeff Duncan (chairman of the Subcommittee on the Western Hemisphere) presiding.

Mr. DUNCAN. A quorum being present, the subcommittee will come to order.

I would now like to recognize myself for an opening statement.

And this is a joint subcommittee hearing between Asia-Pacific and the Western Hemisphere Subcommittees, and so we will allow opening statements from both chairmen as well as ranking members.

In 1793, President George Washington warned a young America that a reputation of weakness could lead us to a loss of America's rank among nations and that if we desired a secure peace it must be known that we are at all times ready for war. Washington also believed a uniform and well-digested plan was vital to meeting these objectives.

While the need for strategic planning to pursue a position of strength and keep the peace finds relevance today, the United States seems to have forgotten Washington's counsel. Broken promises, faded red lines, budget constraints, a lack of support for traditional allies, and an increasing reliance on tactics rather than strategy have communicated U.S. weakness to a watching world.

In 2013, Secretary John Kerry affirmed that the era of the Monroe Doctrine is over, effectively putting other countries, such as China, on notice that the United States would no longer contend their actions in our neighborhood, the Western Hemisphere.

In contrast to Roosevelt's policy of the Good Neighbor in 1933, the U.S. has drifted instead toward benign neglect toward the very countries that have the greatest potential to impact the daily lives of the American people—those in Latin America and the Caribbean. China has taken notice, and China has stepped up into this vacuum of leadership.

Today, China is weaving an intricate web of alliances in the Western Hemisphere through a vast array of diplomatic, economic, and military ties with multiple countries in the region. Although

(1)

the United States remains the largest trading partner for Latin America—and I want to emphasize this—China is now the region's second-largest trading partner and has free-trade agreements with Chile, Peru, and Costa Rica.

This year, China hosted the first-ever China-CELAC summit in Beijing for Latin American and Caribbean nations. This organization expressly excludes both Canada and the United States.

Since 2005, China has provided over $100 billion in credit to the region. Last year, China announced it would give nearly $35 billion in loans to the region in coming years. And, this year, China promised its investment in the region would hit $250 billion over the next 10 years.

These are not just empty assurances. According to the Inter-American Dialogue, China has provided 16 loans valued at over $56 billion to Venezuela, 10 loans valued at $22 billion to Brazil, 10 loans valued at $19 billion to Argentina, and 12 loans valued at almost $11 billion to Ecuador.

In particular, Chinese banks have effectively provided a lifeline to these governments, whose economic mismanagement and corruption prevent them from accessing Western institutions. In return, China receives oil, in the case of both Venezuela and Ecuador. In addition, China has been buying up land and companies in the region, investing heavily in infrastructure and ports, as well as gobbling up a lot of rare earth minerals.

From 2008 to 2012, the 10 largest Chinese mergers and acquisitions occurred in Brazil and Argentina, and other deals have occurred in Ecuador, Venezuela, and Peru.

Of significant interest are two specific infrastructure projects: First, a proposed Chinese-funded and Chinese-controlled Nicaragua Canal, estimated to cost nearly $7 billion, which would rival the Panama Canal and provide greater access for Chinese ships and potentially submarines to the waters near U.S. shores. Second, a Chinese-funded Twin Ocean railroad project connecting Peru and Brazil would also project greater Chinese influence and presence in Latin America.

On a more troubling front, Brazil has provided the Chinese with access to its satellite tracking facilities, which could allow China to gain a more comprehensive picture of the flight paths of U.S. satellites.

In addition, Chinese security ties to the region continue to deepen, with the Chinese arms sales to Bolivia, Venezuela, Ecuador, and Argentina. Reportedly, China has even expanded its arms sales beyond traditional nation-states through providing military-caliber weapons to non-state actors such as the FARC terrorist organization in Colombia and drug trafficking organizations in Mexico. This activity has only served to increase the number of weapons in the hands of paramilitary forces and transnational criminal networks.

It should be of grave concern to all Americans that the Chinese maintain a military presence in Cuba, specifically Lourdes, Bejucal, and Santiago de Cuba, all of which were former Soviet-era monitoring facilities.

Clearly, China has big plans right here in our own hemisphere. And what are we doing about it?

Traditional thinking about China's engagement in the Western Hemisphere was that it was largely being done to counter diplomatic efforts in Taiwan and the region or as a way of paying for extractives or buying energy commodities to fuel their ever-expanding economy.

Some have complained that China uses the region as a dumping ground for goods, such as steel, textiles, footwear, consumer electronics, and tires, and a visit to the marketplaces of the Caribbean and South America would seem to confirm some of those suspicions.

Chinese companies operating in the region often bring their own workers, which they have no real effect on economic growth or jobs in places where they operate, creating a source of friction between China and the countries in the region.

So, in conclusion, the U.S. cannot continue to simply ignore China's presence in this hemisphere. The U.S. must engage more deeply in a sustained way with countries in the Western Hemisphere. It should serve as a jarring wake-up call that just a few days ago five Chinese Navy ships were spotted off the coast of Alaska.

This hearing will be a comprehensive overview of China's activities in the Western Hemisphere and consider how the U.S. can better balance those actions with more effective engagement in the region. So I look forward to hearing from today's expert witnesses.

And, with that, I will turn to the ranking member, Mr. Sires from New Jersey, for any opening statement he may have. And then I will come to the gentleman from Arizona.

So, Mr. Sires, you are recognized.

Mr. SIRES. Thank you, Mr. Chairman.

Good afternoon. Thank you to our witnesses for being here today.

Today, we are examining China's continuing effort to assert influence in Latin America and in the Caribbean.

Over the past decade, China's engagement with Latin America has grown significantly, both economically and diplomatically. Chinese leaders have made several trips throughout the region, including Argentina, Brazil, Venezuela, Colombia, and Cuba.

Their engagement comes, by the way, with foreign direct investment, loans, and increased economic ties. Specifically, they have pledged $250 billion in investment in the region over the next 10 years. China's interest in the region is a result of their constant search for new markets to procure natural resources such as various oils and minerals and agricultural products to feed their domestic needs. Over the past 12 years, trade between Latin America and China has grown from $17 billion to $262 billion. By many estimates, China is the third-largest source of foreign direct investment in Latin America and the Caribbean.

While this can mean greater investment for an emerging Latin American economy and a boost in trade with the region, there are also pitfalls. Chinese investments come with baggage—with the baggage of dubious funding, environmental disregard, and poor labor and health conditions for workers.

Proposed agreements like the $50 billion, 172-mile canal in Nicaragua risk displacing indigenous communities, destroying ecological preserves, and isn't guaranteed to be completed. Mines and factories run by Chinese companies have reported dangerous working conditions, where laborers are overworked, mistreated, and constantly operating in unsafe environments.

For too many years, the United States has focused on other parts of the world, which has led to neglect our own neighborhood. While many have viewed China's increasing engagement in the region as a positive contributor to the region's economic growth, we must remain vigilant of what the long-term consequences might be and reaffirm our own commitment to the region. If China wants to continue to engage our neighbors, we must insist that they comply with international labor, health, and environmental standards.

I look forward to hearing from our panelists.

And thank you.

Mr. DUNCAN. Mr. Salmon, the former chairman of the Western Hemisphere Subcommittee in the last Congress, now-chairman of the Asia-Pacific Subcommittee, he is recognized for 5 minutes.

Mr. SALMON. I am a lot of former things, and I am not going to admit to them all today.

But I would like to thank my good friend Chairman Duncan for convening this joint hearing with me today on China's presence and influence in Latin America and the Caribbean, what I believe to be an understudied yet strategically important trend. I am glad we have a distinguished panel here today to help shed light on this very important issue. We are here today to examine the extent of Chinese political, economic, and military influence in the region, as well as how that may affect U.S. strategic interests.

China's bilateral trade with this hemisphere grew from $15 billion in 2001 to $288.9 billion in 2013. These numbers are staggering and indicative of China's dedication to bolstering its presence in the region.

This January, China pledged to invest $250 billion in Latin America over the next 10 years, serving China's strategic interests of securing access to energy, agriculture, and consumer markets and serving developing Latin American countries' needs for infrastructure development and technological innovation.

While China's presence in Latin America and the Caribbean has been largely limited to trade and investment, there is a movement toward greater military relationships. Nuclear cooperation, shared space assets, and arms sales not only provide China with economic and military leverage in the region but also may expand China's ability to mitigate one of our major advantages: Our relative geographic isolation.

China will continue to allege that it has no foreign bases, meaning that their military posture is inherently defensive. But China's non-explicitly military partnerships with countries in strategic geographic locations like Brazil to share space and satellite assets for Earth observation may raise some eyebrows. ''No foreign bases'' does not mean ''no foreign presence,'' and we should be wary of any potential military implications of Chinese presence in our neighborhood.

In lending billions of dollars to service legitimate needs in developing countries in the Western Hemisphere, China has secured not only lucrative contracts but also diplomatic support. In the 1970s and the 1980s, China made similar inroads in economic assistance to Africa, propelled by the mutual benefit of resources for China and development of African nations. Today, Chinese infrastructure has expanded throughout the continent, and its presence there dominates.

China's involvement in Africa has also marked many African nations' turn-away from formally recognizing Taiwan. In the Western Hemisphere, we currently have 12 states out of 22 total that have formal diplomatic relations with Taiwan, including Nicaragua, Paraguay, and Haiti. Consider China's political benefits from stronger relations with Latin America and the Caribbean countries and what that would mean for the recognition of Taiwan. I am wary of whether China leverages its economic and political sway to further isolate Taiwan.

China's growing economic, trade, military, and diplomatic relationships with countries in Latin America and the Caribbean certainly have implications for U.S. foreign engagement in the region. We welcome China's presence in the region and hope that they will yield mutual benefit for all countries involved. However, we hope this does not come at the expense of the rule of law and good governance and further entrenching inequality, corruption, illicit commerce, and violence.

As the United States continues to look eastward toward Asia, a vital part of our strategic economic future, we must not forget the relationship with our closest neighbors. I look forward to the hearing today about China's strategy within the Western Hemisphere and how we can more effectively manage our presence and our strategy and balance our relationship with our neighbors in the region and China.

Thanks a lot, and I yield back my time.

Mr. DUNCAN. Thank you, Chairman Salmon, for your great leadership and work on these issues in both hemispheres. And it is so important to the American people, so I appreciate that.

Before I recognize you, the bio for each of the witnesses was provided beforehand; I am not going to read that.

You have a lighting system in front of you. We are going to try to maintain a 5-minute rule. If you will, when it gets to yellow, just start trying to wrap up. When it gets to red, we are going to allow a little leeway, but we are going to move on.

So I will go ahead and recognize Dr. Ellis first for 5 minutes. And thank you for being here.

STATEMENT OF EVAN ELLIS, PH.D., AUTHOR, CHINA ON THE GROUND IN LATIN AMERICA

Mr. ELLIS. Thank you very much, Chairman Duncan, Chairman Salmon, Ranking Member Sires, distinguished committee members. Thank you very much for the opportunity to share my analysis with you today. I will summarize my written remarks for the committee.

Chinese engagement with Latin America, while producing some benefits for some actors in the region, is generating negative consequences, and not only for the region but also for the strategic position of the United States. Moreover, these consequences are evolving but not abating with China's current economic deceleration.

PRC trade with the hemisphere today is 20 times greater than it was in 2001, with China primarily purchasing low-value-added commodities while selling higher-value-added manufactured products and services. China has also loaned more than $119 billion to the region since 2005, with approximately three-quarters going to Argentina and the regimes of ALBA.

The physical presence of Chinese companies in the region has taken off in the last 5 years, particularly in mining and petroleum, construction, manufacturing, telecommunications, logistics, and banking. This presence has given China a greater stake in the internal affairs of the countries in which they operate.

With Taiwan, the PRC has generally honored its 2008 informal agreement not to woo countries, recognizing the others to change their diplomatic position. Yet leaders of countries recognizing Taiwan has regularly expressed interest in establishing relations with the PRC. Thus, if current Taiwan-ROC rapprochement breaks down, I believe that the PRC could rapidly eliminate the remaining basis of ROC diplomatic legitimacy in the hemisphere.

I see the near-term objectives of the PRC in the hemisphere as principally economic, yet no less impactful for the U.S. and the region. Primary products: Food stuffs, markets, and technology.

China's President Xi has clearly engaged the hemisphere more boldly than his predecessors, including important trips in May 2013 and July 2014. The latter included the first China-CELAC summit and, indeed, as Chairman Duncan pointed out, an important Chinese choice to frame its multilateral engagement with the hemisphere around an institution that excludes the United States and Canada.

The current deceleration of the Chinese economy is likely to decrease PRC commodity investments and the value of commodity imports but will also likely expand Chinese efforts to sell its goods and services to the region and to pursue more loan-backed infrastructure projects, increasing tensions in an already-troubled relationship.

I am concerned that the PRC engagement is indirectly undermining democracy and good governance in the region, as loans to populist regimes weaken the accountability of their leaders to citizens and institutions and facilitate corruption.

In addition, PRC military activities in the Western Hemisphere, as acknowledged, are significant and growing. Chinese defense conglomerates, such as Norinco, are selling increasingly capable military goods to an ever-broader array of clients. In addition to the well-known sales to Venezuela, Ecuador, and Bolivia, the Peruvian Army just last month received 27 Chinese artillery vehicles, while Argentina plans to purchase Chinese ocean patrol vessels and armored personnel carriers, among other items.

Chinese military personnel attend courses in Colombia's Tolemaida military base and at Brazil's Jungle Warfare School in Manaus. The PLA has progressed from participation in multilateral forces, such as MINUSTAH in Haiti, to bilateral engagements, including a November 2010 medical exercise with Peru and the December 2011 deployment of its hospital ship, Peace Ark, to the Caribbean. In October 2013, for the first time, Chinese warships conducted combat exercises in the region, including engagements with Chile, Argentina, and Brazil.

My recommendations to the committee respectfully include: Number one, working with our regional partners to strengthen their government institutions for engaging with the PRC so that all get a fair and constructive deal; two, ratifying an effective transpacific partnership open to China in the future is one step in constructing a multilateral rule-of-law-based regime across the Pacific; three, facilitating ties between the Western Hemisphere and Asian partners who share our values, including Japan, South Korea, Australia, and India; four, expanding theater security cooperation to bolster the U.S. position as partner of choice in the region; five, prioritizing a functional inter-American system in which the OAS and not CELAC or UNASUR is the multilateral vehicle to engage China and resolve regional security issues; six, articulating a clearer vision of what the U.S. stands for in the hemisphere and why the U.S. approach best advances broad-based development, prosperity, and human dignity.

Respectfully, the U.S. cannot and should not block China-Latin American engagement, but we must, I feel, work to ensure that it is consistent with our own security, while advancing the wellbeing of those with whom we share this hemisphere.

Thank you very much for your time.

[The prepared statement of Mr. Ellis follows:]

R. Evan Ellis, Ph.D.

Research Professor of Latin American Studies

Carlisle Barracks, PA

Testimony to the Joint Hearing of the

Subcommittee on the Western Hemisphere

and the

Subcommittee on Asia and the Pacific

Foreign Affairs Committee

U.S. House of Representatives

Thursday, September 10, 2015

"China's Activities in the Americas"

Chairman Duncan, Chairman Salmon, ranking member Sires, ranking member Sherman, distinguished committee members, thank you for the opportunity to share my views with you today regarding the activities of the People's Republic of China (PRC) in the Western Hemisphere.

While I am a Research Professor at the U.S. Army War College Strategic Studies Institute, I am here today in my personal capacity and, as such, these views are my own and do not represent the position of the Army War College, the U.S. Army, or the Department of Defense.

Overview

The expanding engagement by the PRC with the Western Hemisphere during the past decade is well known, if often mis-characterized. Such engagement is primarily, but not exclusively, economic in nature, and under the right circumstances, could advance the development, prosperity, and even security of the region. Yet while producing *some benefits* for *some actors*, Chinese engagement with the region is also generating significant negative consequences, and is undermining the strategic position of the U.S., in the Western Hemisphere. My remarks are focused on those challenges, and the ways that the U.S. government can work with our Latin American and Caribbean partners to address them.

From the acceptance of the PRC into the World Trade Organization in 2001, until present, PRC bilateral trade with the hemisphere grew by a factor of almost twenty, from $15 billion in 2001 to $288.9 billion in 2013,[1] with China primarily purchasing low value added commodities from the region, such as iron, copper, and soybeans, and in return, selling it a broad array of manufactured products and services, including not only textiles, shoes, and toys, but also higher value-added consumer appliances, cars, tractors, telecommunication equipment, infrastructure projects, military goods, and even space launch services.

Although some commodity exporters such as Chile, Brazil, Peru, and Venezuela have run trade surpluses with the PRC, the overall balance of trade with the region has increasingly tilted in China's favor,[2] with economic problems in the PRC, and globally, decreasing the value of Latin American commodity exports to China, while PRC-based companies with ever more capable products and services, and growing capabilities for doing business in the region, increasingly penetrate its markets,[3] and displace its exports from third markets such as the United States.[4]

The expansion of Chinese trade with Latin America also coincided with a significant growth of Chinese loans to the region, particularly to the nations of ALBA, Argentina, and the Caribbean. Between 2005 and 2013, leading Chinese financial institutions loaned $119 billion to the region, far more than the corresponding total from the

International Monetary Fund and the World Bank.[5] Of these funds, almost three-quarters went to Argentina, Venezuela and Ecuador, supporting efforts by relatively anti-U.S. regimes in those countries to divorce themselves from Western governments and financial institutions. An important portion of these loans also went for projects in the Caribbean, whose small bureaucracies and troubled economies made them willing to accept the government-to-government deals and the use of a principally Chinese labor force to execute the infrastructure projects paid for by those loans.

Beginning in approximately 2010, Chinese engagement with the region also shifted from one dominated principally by trade, to one in which Chinese companies operated on the ground in the region, in select sectors such as mining and petroleum, agriculture, construction, manufacturing, telecommunication, logistics and banking.[6]

The PRC has been relatively open about what it seeks in the region. In January 2015, during the ministerial level summit between the PRC and the Community of Latin American and Caribbean States (CELAC), China advanced a "roadmap" for its relationship with the region, highlighting six "fields" as cooperation priorities, consistent with its activities in the region to date: energy and resources, infrastructure construction, agriculture, manufacturing, scientific and technological innovation, and information technologies."[7]

Yet the PRC and its companies have also frequently been less than transparent in pursuing those objectives. Moreover, it is not clear that the PRC believes that its pursuit of economic objectives in Latin America and the Caribbean is best supported by a region with strong regulatory institutions, competitive public procurement, and a close relationship with the United States.[8]

To some degree, the sectoral concentration of Chinese initiatives in Latin America and the Caribbean resembles that in Africa, characterized by proposed large-scale infrastructure projects which would facilitate PRC access to the region's resources and markets. Prominent examples of the PRC approach in the Western Hemisphere include both projects openly embraced by the Chinese government, such as a proposed railroad link from Bayovar, Peru to Açu, Brazil, as well as projects more nebulously tied to the Chinese government, such as the Nicaragua Canal.

China's new physical presence "on the ground," in the region has given Chinese companies and their government a vastly expanded stake in the internal dynamics of the countries where they operate, as they have dealt with local governments on issues from bids for public projects, to expropriating land, to receiving environmental approvals for construction projects, to favorable treatment on taxation issues.

Beyond governments, the new physical presence of Chinese companies in the region has forced them to engage with local labor forces, contractors, communities, competitors, social groups, and others impacted by their projects.

The Chinese physical presence in the region has also raised the issue of ensuring security for Chinese operations and personnel. Violence against Chinese-operated oil fields in Tarapoa[9] and Orellana[10] Ecuador in 2006 and 2007-2009, against the Colquiri mine in Potosi, Bolivia in 2012,[11] against the Patuca III dam project in Honduras in 2013,[12] and in Caquetá, Colombia in 2011, to include the kidnapping of three Chinese oil workers,[13] are prominent examples, raising questions for the Chinese regarding use of private security, and possibly expanded security relationships in the region, in order to protect Chinese interests.

Particularly in the Caribbean basin, increased commerce, illegal migration, and workers brought in for construction projects have also expanded Chinese populations in the region, and has generated frictions with non-Chinese communities, including in violence against Chinese in Papitam and Maripaston (Suriname) in 2009 and 2011,[14] in Buenos Aires in 2013, and significant protests against Chinese shopkeepers, in Santo Domingo in July 2013.[15]

An ever-more powerful and confident PRC has become increasingly assertive in advocating for the protection of overseas Chinese.[16] When Jamaican Prime Minister Portia Simpson-Miller visited the PRC in August 2013, for example, Chinese premier Li Keqiang placed the issue of criminal violence against Chinese Jamaicans on the table, obligating Simpson-Miller to implement a special program of police protection for the Chinese community.[17]

With respect to Republic of China (ROC), the PRC appears to have generally honored its informal 2008 agreement with the Taiwanese government of Ma Ying-jeou to suspend efforts to suspend efforts to change the diplomatic posture of Latin American and Caribbean governments with respect to diplomatic recognition of the PRC vice the ROC.

Yet virtually all diplomatic communiques between the PRC and the governments of the region that recognize it include language reaffirming support for the "one china" policy, and for the PRC position on Tibet.[18]

Moreover, presidents of Latin American countries which do not recognize the PRC, including Fernando Lugo,[19] Ricardo Martinelli,[20] Porfirio Lobo,[21] and Mauricio Funes[22] among others, have regularly, if unofficially, expressed interest in recognizing the PRC.

Beyond political leaders, PRC-based companies such as Sinohydro in Honduras, and the Chinese international trade promotion office (CCPIT), have been increasingly active in countries recognizing the ROC, suggesting that, were the "diplomatic truce" between the ROC and the PRC to break down, the PRC could rapidly put the remnants of Taiwan's diplomatic legitimacy in the Western Hemisphere in jeopardy.

China's Approach in the Hemisphere

China's President Xi Jinping has engaged the hemisphere in a far bolder fashion than his predecessor Hu Jintao. In his first trip to the region, in May 2013, just two months after assuming the Presidency, Xi visited three countries in the region, all in close proximity to the United States: Costa Rica, Trinidad and Tobago, and Mexico.

President Xi's next trip to the region, in July 2014, was even more symbolically challenging to the United States, focusing exclusively on countries with the U.S. has had difficult relations: Cuba, Venezuela, Brazil, and Argentina. The trip further included two strategically significant multilateral engagements: the sixth meeting of the BRICS in

Fortaleza, Brazil, and the first summit of the China-CELAC forum, which demonstrated the PRC's posture of framing its multilateral engagement with the hemisphere with institutions that exclude the United States.

In addition to these two trips, President Hu has also conducted significant interactions with the Presidents of Brazil, Chile, and Mexico on the sidelines of the November 2014 Asia-Pacific Economic Cooperation forum leadership summit in Beijing, and hosted a second, ministerial level forum with the CELAC countries in Beijing, in January 2015.

Beyond President Xi, significant Chinese engagement with the region has also included the trip two months ago by Primer Li Keqiang to Brazil, Colombia, Peru and Chile.[23]

In general, the PRC has adopted a pragmatic, materialistic, politically agnostic approach in pursuit of its objectives in the region. It has focused on bilateral engagements built around loans and investment projects by Chinese companies, complimented by trade agreements, memorandums of understanding, or administrative certifications which "grant access" to the Chinese market for select categories of merchandise, frequently agricultural goods.

Particularly in the ALBA regimes, and in the smaller states of the Caribbean, the Chinese have also advanced their strategic commercial interests through loan funds, tied to infrastructure projects and product purchases from Chinese companies. In Venezuela and Ecuador, Chinese "loans-for-oil" deals have used linked contracts, on one hand to extend credit (often in RMB), through Chinese banks, for goods and services from PRC-based companies, from the purchase of Haier consumer appliances, [24] to the construction of hydroelectric facilities[25] and railroad lines.[26] Repayment of such loans is achieved through the delivery of oil, generally from fields under Chinese control, thus mitigating the risk of providing funds to the high political risk countries in which they are focused.

In the smaller countries of the Caribbean, the Chinese have established "loan funds" such as the Jamaica Development Infrastructure Program.[27] Such funds turn the tables on established public procurement procedures, to China's advantage: While continuing to adhere to local public procurement rules to some degree, the Chinese establish a pool of money, to which the host government comes to the Chinese, with the requirement that such projects must be done primarily by Chinese companies and workers.

China has also applied the "loan fund" concept at the regional level, including a $3 billion fund for projects across the Caribbean,[28] as well as a $35 billion fund for Latin America as a whole,[29] yet to date, such funds have been little utilized.

PRC Objectives toward Latin America and the Caribbean

The near-term strategic objectives of the PRC in the Western Hemisphere are consistent with those in other parts of the world: (1) securing reliable access to primary products, such as petroleum and minerals necessary to sustain Chinese industrial production, capital formation, and urbanization, (2) reliable access to agricultural goods, particularly animal feeds such as soy and fishmeal, to produce the food to meet the needs of China's 1.35 billion people, (3) reliable access to markets, as Chinese companies expand their capabilities in strategic, high value added sectors such as motor vehicles, electronics, telecommunications, aerospace and defense, construction, finance, and logistics, and (4) access to technology, often through commercial partnerships, to support advances in the aforementioned sectors, and indirectly, an economically diverse, prosperous, and powerful Chinese state.[30]

The fact that such objectives are principally economic does not lessen the challenges that they present for Latin America and the Caribbean, the position of the U.S. in the region, or U.S. efforts to advance an agenda of democracy, human rights, market-oriented economies, and good governance.

Impact of PRC Engagement on U.S. and Regional Interests

While Chinese loans, purchases of Latin American primary products and foodstuffs, investments, and sales of products and services benefit a limited number of sectors and economic interests, they also indirectly contribute to inequality, corruption, violence, and environmental problems, while undermining democracy and the rule of law in the region.[31]

With respect to economic impacts, Chinese imports from the region concentrate primarily on extractive industries and agricultural goods, acquired at their lowest possible point on the value added chain (for example, the acquisition of soybeans rather than soil oil, iron ore, rather than steel or cars, and crude petroleum, rather than refined products).[32] In addition to the Chinese purchasing strategy, the concentration of Chinese investment and loans in these same primary product sectors, to include investments in, and loans for the infrastructure projects that facilitate resource extraction and market access, reinforces the region's concentration on low-value-added extractive activities.[33]

Reciprocally, Chinese exports to the region focus on higher value added consumer and intermediate goods, competing with and adversely affecting similar industries in Latin America and the Caribbean in both domestic markets, as well as in third markets such as the United States.

The current slowing of the PRC economy promises to make such tendencies even more painful for the region, with lower Chinese commodity demand decreasing the net value to the region of Chinese commodity purchases, while weakness in Chinese domestic markets for consumer products and construction projects is likely to push Chinese banks and companies even more aggressively into Latin America and other parts of the world, in search of opportunities.

Expanded commerce between the PRC and Latin America and the Caribbean also multiplies opportunities for trans-pacific organized crime, including contraband goods and other illicit flows.[34] As illustrated by the network exposed during the February 2014 arrest of Mexican narcotraffickers "El Chapo" Guzman, the PRC and India are the two principal sources for precursor chemicals for drugs such as methamphetamines, produced in Latin America for export to the US market.[35] Reciprocally, Chinese companies are key purchasers of metals illicitly extracted from the region as scrap and through informal mining, in places like Michoacán, Mexico, and Madre de Dios, Peru.[36]

Chinese companies have also been implicated in the supply of arms to the Latin American black market, including the March 2015 detention in Cartagena, by Colombian authorities, of a ship traveling from the PRC to Cuba, carrying a large, concealed stash of black powder and other military goods,[37] and the illicit purchase of 4,000 small arms from the Chinese arms company NORINCO by Colombian narcotrafficker Javier Antonio Calle Serna, using the forged signature of then Colombian Commander and Chief General Freddy Padilla.[38]

The expansion of the Chinese business and financial presence in Latin America and the Caribbean has also proliferated opportunities for trans-Pacific money laundering. While the payment of fines by HSBC for laundering money for Mexico's Sinaloa Drug Cartel is the best known case,[39] anecdotal reports have emerged of the Brazilian gang First Capital Command,[40] and other Latin American criminal organizations, using Chinese banks and businesses for their laundering operations.

Trans-pacific criminal ties are an emerging threat which are likely to expand in coming years with emerging PRC-Latin America commerce, particularly since overwhelmed Latin American and Caribbean police forces lack the language skills and technical contacts in the PRC to effectively investigate cases and combat groups with trans-pacific ties.[41]

Beyond such adverse effects, PRC engagement in the region is also undermining democracy and good governance, as well as the Organization of American States (OAS)-led Interamerican system, through Chinese loans, investments, and commodity purchases that sustain the lives of populist regimes, and with them, their questionable adherence to norms of democracy, respect for private property and the rule of law, as well as their efforts (in conjunction with regional powers such as Brazil), to replace the inter-American system with structures such as UNASUR and CELAC, which exclude the US and Canada from a voice in the hemisphere.

According to the most authoritative academic database on Chinese loans to the region, 75% of the $119 billion that Chinese banks have provided to the region between 2005 and 2019 went to the nations of ALBA and Argentina.[42]

As an example of how China's resources has helped to extend the life of populist governments, the PRC provided $4 billion to Venezuela prior to the October 2012 presidential election,[43] allowing its "Bolivarian Socialist" government to expand spending to increase electoral performance. The Ecuadoran government received a commitment for a $1.4 billion loan three months prior to the March 2013 election, and although the money was technically not disbursed until after that election, Ecuador's anticipation of the funds arguably enabled its government to more freely use other funds during the campaign.[44] Similarly, the $7.5 billion in new Chinese loan commitments to Ecuador made in January 2015 helps the country to cover a serious 2015 and 2016 budget shortfalls[45] brought about by sustained low international petroleum prices.

Most recently, the PRC has committed to provide $10 billion in new funds to Venezuela. The money includes a $5 billion loan through the Heavy Investment Fund, which is likely to be delivered in the October-November timeframe,[46] as well as a separate $5 billion loan, agreed to during President Maduro's state visit to the PRC last week, which will be used to help expand petroleum production in oilfields controlled by the Chinese.[47] Both will thus be available to the embattled Maduro government during the run-up to the December 6th mid-term elections in that country.

Aside from their direct political benefits, in both the ALBA regimes and in other recipients of Chinese loans and investment, these resources have arguably undercut the leverage of Western governments and institutions such as the Interamerican Development Bank and World Bank, in advancing transparency, rule of law, and market-based lending practices.

China's willing to pour capital into Argentina and the countries of ALBA has created the illusion for their leaders that they can ignore long-established norms regarding the treatment of international creditors and investors by turning to Chinese loans, investments, and revenue streams. Moreover, by facilitating access to funds with fewer overt requirements for Western-style transparency and accountability, Chinese resources have arguably weakened the accountability of populist leaders to their populations and institutions, and have facilitated the growth of corruption and poor governance in the region.

In addition, by extending the political and financial viability of these regimes, Chinese resources have indirectly facilitated their hosting of other extra-hemispheric actors with a far more openly adversarial posture toward the US, allowing Venezuela, for example, to bring Iranian "Qods" paramilitary forces into the region,[48] or supporting the solvency of anti-U.S. regimes with which Russia could negotiate to secure access for its military aircraft and warships to airfields in ports in the region, and possibly even intelligence gathering facilities, such as the re-opening Russia's US-oriented intelligence gathering facility in Lourdes, Cuba.[49]

PRC activities in strategically important sectors such as telecommunications and space also raise concerns for the U.S. and the region, particularly due to the concentration of such activities in the ALBA regimes, Argentina, and Brazil, with whom diplomatic relations have been strained.

To date, the PRC has developed and launched two satellites for Venezuela and one for Bolivia, and has co-developed and launched four satellites for Brazil under the CBERS program.[50] Follow-on satellites for Brazil,[51] Bolivia,[52] and Venezuela[53] are reportedly in the works, as well as the development and launch of Nicaragua's first satellite by the Chinese defense communications company Xinwei,[54] whose principal shareholder, Wang Jing, is the Chinese billionaire behind the Nicaragua Canal project.

The PRC has also has constructed a space communications facility in Neuquén, Argentina, which has generated concern in the region due to the secrecy surrounding the enabling agreement between the PRC and the Argentine government, and the limited access of Argentines to the PRC-operated facility, despite being located on Argentine territory.[55]

PRC Military Activities in the Hemisphere

The PRC has also expanded its military activities in Latin America and the Caribbean to a far greater extent than is commonly recognized, with potentially adverse impacts on the strategic position of the U.S. in the hemisphere as both a partner of choice, and in a possible future conflict with the PRC.

Just as PRC-based manufacturers are moving up the value added chain into sectors such as autos, heavy equipment, and electronics, Chinese defense companies are also selling increasingly capable military goods to an ever-broader array of clients in Latin America and the Caribbean. Particularly in the last decade, defense sales and gifts by Chinese companies in Latin America and the Caribbean have expanded from clothing and small arms, to advanced weapons systems such as fighter aircraft, radars, armored combat vehicles, and military ships. The client base for the Chinese defense industry in Latin America and the Caribbean has similarly expanded beyond Venezuela, to include sales to Bolivia, Ecuador, Trinidad and Tobago, Peru and Argentina, among others.[56]

Just last month, the Peruvian army took delivery on the first 27 of an order for 40 Type 90B 122mm Chinese multiple launch rocket vehicles,[57] in addition to previously acquired Chinese Beiben, Dong Feng, and Shaanxi military trucks, munitions, and a failed 2010 deal to acquire Chinese MBT-200 tanks.[58]

The most significant recent PRC advance in military sales to the region, to date, is a commitment, made by the Argentine government in February 2015, to purchase 110 Chinese VN-1 8x8 armored personnel carriers, five 1,800-ton P-18A Malvinas-class ocean patrol vessels (OPVs), and 14 Chengdu Aircraft Corporation (CAC) FC-1 or JF-17 multi-role fighters,[59] although the Argentine military appears to be backing away from the fighter acquisition.[60]

The sale of P-18 OPVs represents a significant advance by Chinese military shipbuilders into the Western hemisphere, building on the groundbreaking 2014 agreement for the delivery of one such ship to Trinidad and Tobago.[61]

Expanding PRC military activities in the region also include training and professional military education (PME).

Members of the Chinese People's Liberation Army (PLA) have, on multiple occasions, received instruction at Colombia's Tolemaida military base, not far from U.S. forces.

The PLA similarly sends officers to Brazil's renowned jungle warfare school in Manaus, among other facilities.

With respect to PME, virtually all of the countries in the region which diplomatically recognize the PRC send personnel to courses at the Institute of Defense Studies, part of China's National Defense University in Champing. Some Latin American militaries also sending personnel to Chinese command and to general staff courses in and around Nanjing, Shijiazhuang, and elsewhere in the PRC.[62]

At the tactical level, Latin American military personnel regularly attend courses in the PRC for the operation and maintenance of the aircraft, vehicles, radars, and other weapons systems that the PRC sells to their militaries.[63] In the space sector, key Venezuelan and Bolivian government management and technical personnel have been trained in the PRC, as part of the collaboration through which the PRC built and launched satellites for their governments, and helped to construct supporting ground control facilities.[64]

The Chinese military is also conducting an increasingly broad array of operations in the Western Hemisphere. The PLA has progressed from participation in *multilateral* humanitarian operations, maintaining a contingent of military police in the MINUSTAH peacekeeping force in Haiti from 2004 through 2012, to increasingly sophisticated *bilateral* engagements. These include an earthquake response exercise, held with Peru in November 2010,[65] as well as the deployment of the PRC hospital ship, *Peace Ark*, to the Caribbean in December 2011.[66] Plans are reportedly in place for the *Peace Arc* to return to the region before the end of 2016.

In addition to such humanitarian activities, in October 2013, during the impasse over the U.S. federal budget, a Chinese naval flotilla with two guided missile frigates crossed the Pacific and conducted combat exercises with the Chilean armed forces,[67] and subsequently, with those of Argentina and Brazil.[68]

While the PLA has not yet openly pursued access to ports, airfields, or bases, or otherwise sought to establish a persistent military presence in the region, its military activities in, and goals toward Latin America and the Caribbean are expanding. Indeed, the official PRC defense strategy white paper, released in May 2015, specifies safeguarding China's overseas interests, and international security cooperation as "strategic tasks" of the nation's armed forces.[69]

Recommendations

The United States must not transform competition with the PRC in the Western Hemisphere into enmity. Yet it cannot turn a blind eye to the impacts of Chinese engagement on the region, and on the U.S. strategic position therein, even if short-term PRC intentions appear mostly benign. The security of the United States is bound to Latin America and the Caribbean through ties of geography, commerce, and family. As such, I respectfully submit that we have a responsibility to our citizens, and to our partners in the hemisphere, to ensure that the region's engagement with extra-hemispheric actors such as the PRC is consistent with U.S. objectives of democracy, development, and good governance there, and of course, the security of the U.S. homeland.

There are a number of steps that the U.S. can take in the near-to-mid-term, with the support of this Congress, to address the challenge of China's expanding presence in the hemisphere.

First, while the United States should not inhibit the nations of the region from maintaining political, economic, and military relations with whom they wish, it can and should help them to obtain the maximum possible benefit from their engagement with the PRC, while avoiding potential pitfalls and negative consequences. Doing so involves supporting and helping to strengthen Latin American and Caribbean institutions dealing with the PRC, including the strengthening of relevant legal frameworks, planning, analysis and negotiating capabilities in the region.

Second, the U.S. must work with its partners in both Asia and Latin America to support a trans-Pacific regime that is governed by the rule of law, and in which all nations, including the PRC, have the opportunity to reap the benefits of their governmental and private sector initiatives. To this end, it is important that Congress support the completion and ratification of an effective Trans Pacific Partnership (TPP), and in the future, expansion of the TPP to accommodate participation by the PRC therein, in recognition of China's role as a key player in the Pacific community.

Beyond the TPP, the U.S. government can also do more to actively promote ties between partners in the hemisphere, and counterpart governments across the Pacific which share U.S. values and strategic interests, including (but not limited to), Japan, South Korea, Australia, and India. Possible facilitating mechanisms include scholarships in U.S. universities for Asian students developing skills for doing business with Latin America, and Latin students similarly seeking to do business in Asia. The U.S. can similarly expand programs to promote connections between Latin American businessmen and those in select Asian countries sharing our values, with through U.S. government-sponsored forums.

With respect to the military, PRC activities in the hemisphere should be carefully monitored, albeit not necessarily opposed; under the appropriate legal framework and conditions of transparency, Chinese military goods and assistance may help the governments of Latin America and the Caribbean to combat the grave problems of organized crime and delinquency that the region faces. Nonetheless, it is important that the U.S. closely monitor such Chinese activities, even while it insists on their transparency. Concurrently, it is important that the U.S. expand and strengthen its own theater security cooperation, including funding spaces in U.S. institutions for professional military education and training, to help ensure the continuing U.S. position as security partner of choice for the region.

Beyond monitoring Chinese activities and expanding U.S. theater security cooperation, those responsible for future planning in NORTHCOM, SOUTHCOM, and other relevant U.S. government organizations, should regularly, and thoroughly evaluate how, in the event of a major conflict, actors such as the PRC could leverage commercial assets and political and military relationships in the Western Hemisphere, to act against the U.S. in the region.

It is also important that the U.S. give more strategic priority to ensuring the functionality of an Interamerican system in which all states in the hemisphere, including the U.S., have a voice, so that the Western Hemisphere can engage the PRC and other extra-regional actors from a position of strength, within a framework of democracy, effective institutions, and the rule of law. The U.S. must make clear to the PRC and other extra-hemispheric actors that privileging CELAC or other multilateral institutions that deliberately exclude the United States and Canada, will be regarded as a hostile act.

Finally, this government must do more to advance a vision of what it stands for, and why the U.S. approach, if not always perfect, is the hemisphere's best bet to advance development, prosperity, and human dignity. In the words of the 2015 Quadrennial Diplomacy and Development Review (QDDR), "America is strongest when our optimism, integrity, ideals and innovation are a model for the world."[70] The U.S. vision should include, but not be limited to, four pillars: democracy, human rights, the rule of law, and freedom from corruption.

While the United States must always be respectful of the sovereignty and individual situations of the governments in the region, it cannot, and should not engage with the PRC in a value-free competition promising material benefits to win the loyalty of those currently in power. Indeed as the Chinese have already learned in Venezuela and Guyana, governments that provide access for benefits today, may not be in power tomorrow, and the governments that follow them may not look positively on particularistic, unjust, or unconstitutional deals that their predecessors have made with stronger states, be it the Chinese, the United States, or others.

The U.S. cannot exclude China from the hemisphere, but we can work respectfully to ensure that engagement advances the well-being of those with whom we share this hemisphere, within the framework of democracy, human rights, and the rule of law.

---

[1] *Direction of Trade Statistics*, International Monetary Fund, June 2014, p. 33.

[2] Based on the *Direction of Trade Statistics Yearbook*, International Monetary Fund, 2014, p. 137.

[3] One of the most comprehensive economic studies regarding the negative impact of competition from the PRC on exports in Latin America and the globe is Débora Bellucci and Célio Hiratuka Módolo, "Impacto da concorrência chinesa em terceiros mercados: uma análise por regiões e por categorias tecnológicas," http://www.anpec.org.br/encontro/2012/inscricao/files_I/i6-9a2f68519249af21127e6ef9db64ea2d.doc.

[4] See, for example, Enrique Dussel Peters and Kevin P. Gallagher, "NAFTA's Uninvited Guest: China and the Disintegration of North American Trade," *CEPAL Review*, No. 110, August 2013, pp. 83-108.

[5] "China-Latin America Finance Database," Interamerican Dialogue, accessed January 18, 2015, http://thedialogue.org/map_list.

[6] For a detailed analysis of China's expanding commercial presence in Latin America and the Caribbean since 2010, see R. Evan Ellis, *China on the Ground in Latin America: Challenges for the Chinese and Impacts on the Region*, New York: Palgrave-Macmillan, 2014. See also *La Inversion Extranjera Directa en America Latina: 10 casos de estudio*, Enrique Dussel Peters, Coord., Mexico City: UNAM, 2014, http://dusselpeters.com/73.pdf.

[7] "Xi Jinping Attends China-Latin America and the Caribbean Summit," Ministry of Foreign Affairs of the People's Republic of China, July 18, 2014, http://www.fmprc.gov.cn/mfa_eng/topics_665678/xjpzxcxjzgjldrdlchwdbxagtwnrlgbjxgsfwbcxzlldrhw/t1176650.shtml.

[8] See, for example, R. Evan Ellis, "The Strategic Relevance of Latin America for the United States." U.S. Army War College Strategic Studies Institute, December 8, 2014, http://strategicstudiesinstitute.army.mil/index.cfm/articles/The-Strategic-Relevance-of-Latin-America/2014/12/08.

[9] "Petrolera china desestima que protesta en Tarapoa haya afectado sus intereses," *El Universo*, November 14, 2006, http://www.eluniverso.com/2006/11/14/0001/9/DDDBC2F740814980A854CA2B3B92CB18.html.

[10] "Matanza en Oriente sería por petroleras," *El Universo*, August 16, 2009, http://www.eluniverso.com/2009/08/16/1/1447/matanza-oriente-seria-petroleras.html.

[11] "Colquiri aún dialoga y denuncian más tomas," *Los Tiempos*, June 9, 2012, http://www.lostiempos.com/diario/actualidad/economia/20120906/colquiri-aun-dialoga-y-denuncian-mas-tomas_184554_391189.html.

25

[12] "Estancadas las obras en la represa hidroeléctrica Patuca III en Honduras," *La Prensa*, August 15, 2013, http://www.laprensa.hn/honduras/apertura/328490-98/estancadas-las-obras-en-la-represa-hidroeléctrica-patuca-iii-en-honduras.

[13] "Secuestran a tres chinos en Caquetá," *El Tiempo,* June 9, 2011, http://www.eltiempo.com/archivo/documento/CMS-9573466.

[14] Ellis, *China on the Ground in Latin America.*

[15] Omar Santana, "Protestan contra "nuevos comerciantes chinos," *Diario Libre,* July 30, 2013, http://www.diariolibre.com.

[16] Ellis, *China on the Ground in Latin America.*

[17] "Police To Ramp Up Security Measures For Chinese Community In Jamaica," *Go Jamaica*, August 27, 2013, http://go-jamaica.com.

[18] See, for example, R. Evan Ellis, "Latin America's Foreign Policy as the Region Engages in China," *Security and Defense Studies Review*, Center for Hemispheric Defense Studies, Winter 2014, http://www.academia.edu/10379257/Latin_Americas_Foreign_Policy_as_the_Region_Engages_China.

[19] "Posible relación con China Continental." *ABC Digital*. Asuncion, Paraguay. http://www.abc.com.py. June 7, 2007.

[20] Jenny W. Hsu, "Panama respects Taiwan, China 'truce': ambassador," *Taipei Times*, February 6, 2010, http://www.taipeitimes.com. See also "Taiwan corteja a Martinelli," *La Prensa*, December 27, 2009, http://www.prensa.com/politica/Taiwan-corteja-Martinelli_0_2735726516.html.

[21] "Honduras abrirá relaciones diplomáticas con China," *La Prensa*, December 8, 2009, http://www.laprensa.hn/honduras/536420-97/honduras-abrira-relaciones-diplomaticas-con-china.

[22] "El Salvador anuncia que restablecerá relaciones con Cuba," *Hoy,* March 18, 2009, http://www.hoy.com.ec.

[23] See, for example, R. Evan Ellis, "Premier Li's Trip to Latin America: More, Not Different," *The Manzella Report*, May 23, 2015, http://manzellareport.com/index.php/world/998-li-keqiang-s-latin-america-trip-more-not-different.

[24] "Programa Mi Casa Bien Equipada ofrece 14 mil equipos en Los Próceres," *El Universal*, August 29, 2012, http://www.eluniversal.com.

[25] For a detailed discussion of Chinese hydroelectric projects in Latin America, see R. Evan Ellis, "Are Big Chinese Energy Investments in Latin America a Concern?" *The Manzella Report*, November 23, 2013, http://www.manzellareport.com/index.php/world/781-are-big-chinese-energy-investments-in-latin-america-a-concern. See also Ellis, *China on the Ground in Latin America*.

[26] Two prominent examples are the Bayovar-Açu transcontinental railroad, and the subsequently cancelled Mexico City-Queretaro high-speed rail project. With respect to the transcontinental railroad, see Jonathan Watts, "China's Amazonian railway 'threatens uncontacted tribes' and the rainforest," *The Guardian*, May 16, 2015, http://www.theguardian.com/world/2015/may/16/amazon-china-railway-plan. With respect to the Mexico City-Queretaro railroad, see Clint Richards, "Why China Won Mexico's High-Speed Rail Project," *The Diplomat*, November 4, 2014, http://thediplomat.com/2014/11/why-china-won-mexicos-high-speed-rail-project/.

[27] "Jamaica signs another major infrastructure deal with China," *Stabroek News*, March 11, 2013, http://www.stabroeknews.com/2013/news/regional/03/11/jamaica-signs-another-major-infrastructure-deal-with-china/.

[28] Joshua Goodman, "China's Xi Offers Caribbean Nations $3 Billion in Loans," *Bloomberg*, June 3, 2013, http://www.bloomberg.com/news/articles/2013-06-03/china-s-xi-offers-caribbean-nations-3-billion-in-loans.

[2929] "China offers 35bn fund to finance infrastructure projects in Latin America," *MercoPress*, July 18, 2014, http://en.mercopress.com/2014/07/18/china-offers-35bn-fund-to-finance-infrastructure-projects-in-latin-america.

[30] For a detailed discussion of these objectives, see R. Evan Ellis, *China and Latin America: The Whats and Wherefores*, Boulder, CO: Lynne Rienner Publishers, 2009.

[31] See, for example, R. Evan Ellis, "Chinese Influence on Latin America: Challenges and Opportunities." *Latin American Democracy: Emerging Reality or Endangered Species?*, 2nd Ed, Richard L. Millett, Jennifer S. Holmes, and Orlando J. Perez, eds. Routledge, 2015, pp. 264-279.

[32] Eduardo Daniel Oviedo, "El ascenso de china y sus efectos en la relación con Argentina," *Estudios Internacionales*, No. 180, University of Chile, 2015, pp. 67-90.

[33] For a discussion of the impact of China in moving the region toward a greater concentration on primary product production, see Ottón Solis, "Alba y neoliberalismo: desvestidos por China," *Nación*, September 22, 2012, http://www.nacion.com/archivo/Alba-neoliberalismo-desvestidos-China_0_1294670555.html.

[34] For a detailed discussion, see R. Evan Ellis, "Chinese Organized Crime in Latin America," *Prism*, Vol. 4, No. 1, December 1, 2012, pp. 67-77.

27

35 "Capo mexicano capturado coordinaba el tráfico de drogas de Colombia y China," *Noticias 24*, March 12, 2012, http://www.noticias24.com/internacionales/noticia/33575/capo-capturado-coordinaba-el-trafico-de-droga-de-colombia-y-china/.

36 R, Evan Ellis, *The Strategic Dimension of China's Engagement with Latin America*. William J. Perry Paper. Washington DC: Center for Hemispheric Defense Studies, October 2013, http://chds.dodlive.mil/files/2013/12/pub-PP-ellis.pdf, pp. 122-125.

37 "China dice que carguero detenido en Cartagena llevaba material militar 'ordinario',"*El País*, March 4, 2015, http://www.elpais.com.co/elpais/colombia/noticias/china-dice-carguero-detenido-cartagena-llevaba-material-militar-ordinario.

38 R. Evan Ellis, "New Developments in China-Colombia Engagement," *The Manzella Report*, October 27, 2014, http://www.manzellareport.com/index.php/world/910-new-developments-in-china-colombia-engagement?tmpl=component&print=1&layout=default&page=,

39 Carrick Mollenkamp, "HSBC became bank to drug cartels, pays big for lapses," *Reuters*, December 11, 2012, http://www.reuters.com/article/2012/12/12/us-hsbc-probe-idUSBRE8BA05M20121212.

40 Bruno Riberio, "PCC envia dinheiro do tráfico para Estados Unidos e China," *O Estado de São Paolo*, January 15, 2015, http://sao-paulo.estadao.com.br/noticias/geral,pcc-envia-dinheiro-do-trafico-para-estados-unidos-e-china,1619985.

41 For a more detailed discussion of this challenge, see Ellis, *The Strategic Dimension of China's Engagement with Latin America*, pp. 117-134.

42 "China-Latin America Finance Database."

43 "Programa Mi Casa Bien Equipada ha vendido 850 mil equipos," *El Universal*, February 7, 2012, http://www.eluniversal.com/economia/120207/programa-mi-casa-bien-equipada-ha-vendido-850-mil-equipos.

44 "Ecuador recibe $1.400 millones de un crédito chino," *La Republica*, February 26, 2013, http://www.larepublica.ec/blog/economia/2013/02/26/ecuador-recibe-1-400-millones-de-un-credito-chino/.

45 Ed Adamczyk, "China agrees to financing for Ecuador, Venezuela," *United Press International*, January 8, 2014, http://www.upi.com/Top_News/World-News/2015/01/08/China-agrees-to-financing-for-Ecuador-Venezuela/6751420741127/.

46 For an in-depth discussion of the deepening crisis in Venezuela and the role of PRC funds in sustaining the regime, see R. Evan Ellis, "The Approaching Implosion of

Venezuela and Strategic Implications for the United States," Carlisle Barracks, PA: U.S. Army War College Strategic Studies Institute, July 7, 2015, http://www.strategicstudiesinstitute.army.mil/index.cfm/articles/the-approaching-implosion-of-venezuela/2015/07/10 ,

[47] "China dará préstamo para subir producción petrolera," *El Universal*, September 2, 2015, http://www.eluniversal.com/economia/150902/china-dara-prestamo-para-subir-produccion-petrolera.

[48] "Countering Iran in the Western Hemisphere Act of 2012," H.R. 3783, 112th Congress, 2nd Session, January 3, 2012, http://www.gpo.gov/fdsys/pkg/BILLS-112hr3783enr/pdf/BILLS-112hr3783enr.pdf.

[49] "Russia with plans for military bases in Nicaragua, Cuba and Venezuela," *MercoPress*, February 17, 2014, http://en.mercopress.com/2014/02/27/russia-with-plans-for-military-bases-in-nicaragua-cuba-and-venezuela.

[50] "Brasil y China negocian la construcción de un nuevo satélite de la familia CBERS para ser lanzado en tres años," *Defensa*, January 14, 2015, http://www.defensa.com/index.php?option=com_content&view=article&id=14403:brasil-y-china-negocian-la-construccion-de-un-nuevo-satelite-de-la-familia-cbers-para-ser-lanzado-en-tres-anos&catid=141:espacio&Itemid=314.

[51] Caleb Henry, "China Launches CBERS 4 Satellite, Plans Future Launch Vehicles," *Satellite Today*, December 8, 2014, http://www.satellitetoday.com/launch/2014/12/08/china-launches-cbers-4-satellite-plans-future-launch-vehicles/.

[52] "Postergan el satélite 'Bartolina'" *Los Tiempos*, July 24, 2015, http://www.lostiempos.com/diario/actualidad/economia/20150724/postergan-el-sat%C3%A9lite-%E2%80%9Cbartolina%E2%80%9D_309508_684878.html.

[53] "Venezuela tendrá un tercer satélite," *Ultimas Noticias*, July 21, 2014, http://www.ultimasnoticias.com.ve/noticias/actualidad/politica/venezuela-tendra-un-tercer-satelite.aspx.

[54] Humberto Galo, "Nicaragua comprará satélite a empresa china." *La Prensa*, September 13, 2012, http://www.laprensa.com.ni/2012/09/13/nacionales/116195-nicaragua-comprara-satelite-a-empresa-china. See also "Nicaragua negotiating satellite purchase with China," *Space Daily*, September 14, 2012, http://www.spacedaily.com/reports/Nicaragua_negotiating_satellite_purchase_with_China_999.html.

[55] "China constructing a satellite tracking station in Argentine Patagonia," *MercoPress*, September 12, 2014, http://en.mercopress.com/2014/09/12/china-constructing-a-satellite-tracking-station-in-argentine-patagonia.

[56] For a detailed discussion of Chinese military activities in the region, see R. Evan Ellis, "Should U.S. be worried about Chinese arms sales in the region?" *Latin America Goes Global*, http://latinamericagoesglobal.org/2015/05/should-u-s-be-worried-about-chinese-arms-sales-in-the-region/, May 11, 2015. See also R. Evan Ellis, "China-Latin America Military Engagement: Good Will, Good Business, and Strategic Position." Carlisle Barracks, PA: U.S. Army War College Strategic Studies Institute, August 2011, http://www.strategicstudiesinstitute.army.mil/pubs/display.cfm?pubID=1077,

[57] Cesar Cruz Tantalean, "Peru receives Chinese tactical MRLs" *IHS Jane's 360*, July 21, 2015, http://www.janes.com/article/53133/peru-receives-chinese-tactical-mrls.

[58] "Gobierno suspende indefinidamente compra del tanque chino MBT-2000," *La Republica*. April 7, 2010, http://www.larepublica.pe/08-04-2010/gobierno-suspenda-indefinidamente-compra-del-tanque-chino-mbt-2000.

[59] "Analysis: China looks to break into Latin American market via Argentina," *IHS Jane's 360*, February 10, 2015, http://www.janes.com/article/48872/analysis-china-looks-to-break-into-latin-american-market-via-argentina.

[60] "La Fuerza Aérea descartó la compra de un caza chino (III)," *Desarrollo y Defensa*, August 29, 2015, http://desarrolloydefensa.blogspot.com.ar/2015/08/la-fuerza-aerea-descarto-la-compra-de.html?m=1.

[61] "China entregará un buque patrullero a Trinidad y Tobago," *Infodefensa*, March 11, 2014, http://www.infodefensa.com/latam/2014/03/11/noticia-china-entregara-buque-patrullero-trinidad-tobago.html.

[62] For examples and a detailed discussion, see Ellis, *The Strategic Dimension of China's Engagement with Latin America*, pp. 93-96.

[63] Ellis, *The Strategic Dimension of China's Engagement with Latin America*. pp. 97-102.

[64] With respect to the training of Venezuelan personnel in the PRC, see James Suggett, "Venezuela to Launch its First Satellite from China in November," *Venezuelanaysis*, August 18, 2008, http://venezuelanalysis.com/news/3729. With respect to the training of Bolivian personnel, see "Presentan a bolivianos que se capacitarán en China para operar el satélite Tupac Katari," *El Diario*, La Paz, Bolivia, October 10, 2012.

[65] "Ejércitos de Perú y China concluyen operación de acción humanitaria conjunta en Lima," *Andina*, November 30, 2010, http://www.andina.com.pe/agencia/noticia-ejercitos-peru-y-china-concluyen-operacion-accion-humanitaria-conjunta-lima-330446.aspx.

[66] There, it conducted medical engagements in Jamaica, Trinidad and Tobago, Cuba and Costa Rica. See "China's Hospital Ship sets sail for Caribbean States," *China*

Radio International, September 27, 2015,
http://english.cri.cn/6909/2011/09/27/2743s660290.htm.

[67] "PLAN's taskforce conducts maritime joint exercise with Chilean Navy," *Ministry of Defense of the People's Republic of China.* Official Website, October 12, 2013, http://eng.mod.gov.cn/TopNews/2013-10/12/content_4470459.htm. See also "Armadas de China y Chile Realizaron Ejercicios Navales," *Noticias FFAA Chile,* October 16, 2013, http://noticiasffaachile.blogspot.com/2013/10/armadas-de-china-y-chile-realizaron.html.

[68] "PLAN taskforce conducts joint maritime exercise with Brazilian Navy," *Ministry of Defense* of the People's Republic of China, Official Website, October 28, 2013, http://eng.mod.gov.cn/DefenseNews/2013-10/28/content_4472787.htm.

[69] "China's Military Strategy," The State Council Information Office of the People's Republic of China, May 26, 2015, http://eng.mod.gov.cn/Database/WhitePapers/index.htm.

[70] *Enduring Leadership in a Dynamic World,* Quadrennial Diplomacy and Development Review 2015, Washington D.C.: U.S. http://www.state.gov/documents/organization/241429.pdf. P. 8.

Mr. DUNCAN. Okay. Is it ''Dussel Peters'' or just ''Peters''?

Mr. DUSSEL PETERS. ''Dussel Peters.''

Mr. DUNCAN. All right. Dr. Dussel Peters is recognized for 5 minutes.

STATEMENT OF ENRIQUE DUSSEL PETERS, PH.D., DIRECTOR, CENTER FOR CHINESE-MEXICAN STUDIES, SCHOOL OF ECONOMICS, NATIONAL AUTONOMOUS UNIVERSITY OF MEXICO

Mr. DUSSEL PETERS. Okay. Thank you very much, Mr. Chairman and members of the subcommittees.

I would like to share with you the work of the last 15 years we have been doing on the Mexico and Latin America-China relationship. And I also invite you to participate next Wednesday in a presentation of a report we will do with the Atlantic Council exactly on this topic, no?

I would like to share with you three topics.

First, the first issue, the increasing relationship of Latin America and China in all the topics that we have been mentioning is no coincidence, which means China has been in the last at least 10 years releasing a group of white papers regarding this relationship. I would invite you to go through the cooperation plan of CELAC and China, the first ministerial meeting that was published in January 2015, which establishes very clear goals regarding trade, investment, infrastructure projects, and funding, respectively.

There is no single Latin American country that so far has established a short-, medium-, and long-term strategy vis-a-vis China. This results in a substantial disadvantage for Latin America.

Second, as you mentioned, China has become the second-largest trading partner of Latin America. Latin America has a huge trade deficit, and particularly relevant is the difference in the group of topics and of products that the region is exporting to China. Less than 5 percent of Latin American exports to China are of medium- and high-technological level. There is a huge gap with what China is exporting to the region, and this has also reflected and explains the region's increasing disenchantment with its most dynamic partner.

Finally, the third topic I would like to share with you is that, while it is well known that China has participated importantly in the NAFTA region and displaced also Mexican exports to the United States, probably the United States has been the main loser in this new triangular relationship between the United States, Latin America, and China.

In the paper I submitted to you, we calculate that 72 percent of the United States exports to Latin America are threatened by Chinese exports. And probably much more important is that, if we assume the share of the United States in Latin American imports of 2001 when China became a member of the World Trade Organization, if we assume the same share of Latin American imports in 2014, the United States would have exported to Latin America more than $145 billion additionally.

If we take this $145 billion in 2014, according to the Department of Commerce, this $145 billion accounts for 840,000 jobs that the United States would have gained, maintaining the same share in

2001. Again, this is a substantial and critical topic not only for Latin America and for Mexico but for the United States.

I finish with two recommendations.

First, I invite very much both subcommittees and the House of Representatives, A, to support, fund, and create academic and private institutions in the United States to promote detailed understanding of a dialogue on the global reemergence of China, especially in Latin America and the Caribbean, since it also affects U.S. trade, production, and employment, especially in manufacturing and particularly in the automobile and auto parts sectors.

Secondly, I invite you to actively participate in and support the important work that has been done in Latin America and the Caribbean on the many issues related to this new triangular relationship. Institutions such as CELAC, the Economic Commission for Latin America and the Caribbean, and the Inter-American Development Bank are some of the institutions where you could participate.

Thank you very much for your time.

[The prepared statement of Mr. Dussel Peters follows:]

Testimony before the Joint Subcommittee Hearing

Subcommittee on the Western Hemisphere and Subcommittee on Asia and the Pacific

Committee on Foreign Affairs

United States House of Representatives

Hearing on China's Advance in Latin America and the Caribbean

September 10, 2015

Submitted by Enrique Dussel Peters, Ph.D.

Director

Center for Chinese-Mexican Studies

School of Economics

National Autonomous University of Mexico

Mr. Chairman, Ranking Member Sires, and Members of the Subcommittees:

Thank you for the opportunity to testify on China's advance in Latin America and the Caribbean. I ask that my full testimony be submitted for the record. My name is Enrique Dussel Peters, and I am a full-time professor at the School of Economics of the National Autonomous University of Mexico, and have been the director of that university's Center for Chinese-Mexican Studies since 2006 and director of the Academic Network of Latin America and the Caribbean on China since 2012.

In both initiatives, as well as in earlier research, we have been working with dozens of research groups and hundreds of researchers, firms, and business organizations, as well as public officials and experts from many countries in Latin America and the Caribbean, particularly in Mexico, on trade and investment issues. As part of this work, we have engaged in a detailed dialogue with Chinese counterparts in the academic, business, and public sectors. Since 2000, research by both institutions and my own personal research have resulted in the publication of dozens of books and articles. Interactions with newspapers and radio and television stations in China, the United States, Europe, and Latin America and the Caribbean have been particularly fruitful. This detailed research and analysis has been accompanied by proposals and policy suggestions, including dozens of specific project proposals for Mexico City and Beijing.

I would like to share with the Members of the Subcommittees an assessment of three issues—(1) China's objectives in Latin America and the Caribbean, (2) China's economic relationship with the region, and (3) Chinese companies' trade and investment activities in Mexico, including as they relate to NAFTA—and recommendations for actions by the U.S. Congress on these issues.

China's objectives in Latin America and the Caribbean

Mr. Chairman, in the last decade, the relationship between Latin America and the Caribbean and China has intensified, particularly regarding trade but also in terms of political, cultural, educational, historical, language-instruction, and investment contacts. This trend is no coincidence, but a result of long-term strategies and policies of the Chinese central government. Its first explicit policy paper on Latin America and the Caribbean was released in 2008; the Cooperation Plan (2015–2019), produced by the first ministerial meeting of the CELAC

(Community of Latin American and Caribbean States)–China Forum in January 2015, is the most detailed and concrete commitment between China and Latin America and the Caribbean.

The Cooperation Plan commits to doubling trade between the region and China to $500 billion annually by 2025 and to more than tripling Chinese foreign direct investment (FDI) to at least $250 billion in the same time frame. It covers infrastructure and transportation, energy and natural resources, industry, science and technology, aviation and aerospace, education and human resources training, as well as tourism and culture. In addition, Chinese and Latin American/Caribbean firms are encouraged to work toward the integration of Latin America and the Caribbean through formal forums (for example on infrastructure, industrial development, and science and technology), many of which oversee a corresponding fund. These strategies go hand-in-hand with other global and regional policies established by the central government of China, also known as the "new Silk Road" and the "one belt, one road" initiative, focusing on international cooperation through infrastructure development (for example, through the recently established Asian Infrastructure Investment Bank).

China's engagement is not limited to the economic field: We are witnessing China's long-term global reemergence in a variety of fields, including militarily and geostrategically. From a Latin American and Caribbean perspective, however, the Cooperation Plan reflects some of the main institutional weaknesses in the region. CELAC only has a *pro tempore* presidency and lacks a secretariat or specialized group of professionals working to fulfill its commitments, even in terms of evaluation. In addition, no Latin American or Caribbean country today has presented a clear and comprehensive strategy toward China in the economic, political, military, educational, and cultural areas. In this regard, China's relatively coherent strategy puts it at a significant advantage.

As a result of China's reemergence, and based on historical and current relationships with the United States, new triangular relationships have developed in the last decade between Latin American and Caribbean countries, the United States, and China.

China's relationship with Latin America and the Caribbean

China is rapidly and profoundly changing Latin American and Caribbean societies and economies, starting with trade and expanding into FDI and massive financing, especially in the following ways:

1. During 2000–2014, China became the region's second largest trading partner after the United States; China's share of Latin American and Caribbean exports increased from 1 percent to 9 percent, while imports from China grew from 2 percent to 16 percent.

2. The region's trade deficit with China has increased substantially, from below $20 billion until the mid-2000s to over $75 billion since 2012. The Caribbean, Central America, and particularly Mexico account for most of this deficit.

3. While Latin American and Caribbean exports to China have increased, they are dominated by low-value-added and low-technology goods. Medium- and high-technology goods account for barely 5 percent of the region's exports to China (compared with 30 to 40 percent of total Latin American and Caribbean exports over the last two decades), while medium- and high-technology goods accounted for more than 60 percent of Chinese exports to Latin America and the Caribbean in the last decade. This gap helps explain the region's increasing disenchantment with its most dynamic trading partner.

4. Latin American and Caribbean exports to China are much more concentrated than exports to any other trading partner: The top three exports to China—ores, oil seed and copper—increased their share of total exports from 50 percent to 72 percent during 2000–2014.

5. Since the late 2000s and particularly since the international crisis of 2007–2008, China has begun a second stage in its relationship with Latin America and the Caribbean, based on FDI and financing. During 2010–2013, China invested on average $10.7 billion annually in Latin America and the Caribbean, with almost 90% going to Argentina, Brazil, and Peru. Chinese companies have actively pursued mergers and acquisitions in the region, especially to acquire raw materials and a share in the corresponding domestic markets (57 percent and 34 percent, respectively, of China's total FDI in Latin America and the Caribbean in 2000–2012). This effort is predominantly (87 percent in the same time period) carried out by publicly owned firms.

6. China is also increasing its financial presence. From 2005 to 2014, loan commitments totaled more than $118 billion. Venezuela alone accounted for more than 50 percent of total loans and 42 percent of infrastructure projects in the region. This rather new Chinese

focus on finance will likely grow substantially, given the expected increase in Chinese infrastructure projects.

Finally, China is competing vigorously with Latin American and Caribbean firms in the United States and with US firms in Latin America and the Caribbean. This has, so far, not been recognized and analyzed sufficiently in the United States. It is apparently widely known that China has displaced Mexico in the US market, but there is insufficient understanding of the massive effects of Chinese competition with US firms in Latin American and Caribbean markets since 2001, when China joined the World Trade Organization. A competitive threat analysis yields the following results:

1. China dramatically increased its share of total US imports during 2001–2014, from 9 percent to 16 percent. Latin America and the Caribbean's share also increased, but less dramatically—from 16 percent to 19 percent.

2. China's share of Latin America and the Caribbean's imports increased sharply, from 3 percent in 2001 to 17 percent in 2014, while the United States' share fell from 46 percent to 32 percent.

3. The impact of this loss of market share in Latin America and the Caribbean on jobs in the United States is significant. It can be estimated as follows: If the US share of the region's imports had remained the same as in 2001 (46 percent), the value of US exports to the region would have been $145 billion higher in 2014. Based on recent estimates by the Department of Commerce (International Trade Administration) of jobs supported per billion dollars of exports, the additional $145 billion would have generated 840,000 jobs in the United States in 2014 alone, all related to manufacturing and 55 percent related to automobiles and auto parts.

While it is true that Latin America and Caribbean–China trade and investment have been booming since 2001, particularly through commodity exports until 2007–2008, it is also true that trade with China has generated massive setbacks for the region, including a significant trade deficit and even greater dependence on exporting raw materials rather than value-added and technology-intensive goods.

The Latin American and Caribbean region has some disadvantages competing with China as exporters to markets such as the United States. However, losses to the United States in its competition with China in the region have been greater, and the effects on trade and jobs have been substantial.

Chinese trade and investment in Mexico

This section focuses on Mexico, rather than the whole of Latin America and the Caribbean. Based on analysis by the Center for Chinese-Mexican Studies, the Academic Network of Latin America and the Caribbean on China, and other public and private institutions, the recent economic relationship between Mexico and China could be summarized as follows:

1. Trade increased during 2001–2014 by a factor of 17; China is Mexico's second trading partner after the United States. Trade, however, is highly unequal: In 2014, each unit exported from Mexico to China corresponded to 11 units imported from China. The share of medium- and high-technology goods in Mexico's exports to China is unique for Latin America, at more than one-third, but this is till significantly below the corresponding share, two-thirds, in Chinese imports to Mexico.

2. During 1999–2014, China invested significantly less in Mexico than in most of the rest of Latin America and the Caribbean, accounting for an accumulated FDI of around $360 million or 0.1 percent of total FDI in Mexico.

3. Unlike in most of Latin America and the Caribbean, Chinese FDI in Mexico has concentrated in manufacturing and services in firms such as Hutchinson Ports, Huawei, Minth, Lenovo, Golden Dragon, and Sinatex. Chinese FDI is qualitatively different from most FDI in Mexico because of the recent establishment of these firms (most of which are less than 10 years old), and because of their problems in complying with NAFTA rules of origin in order to export to the region as a whole, and in particular to find specialized local, national, and regional suppliers and distributors. The learning process of Chinese firms, like that of Mexican firms in China such as Bimbo and Gruma, has been slow and full of misunderstandings on both sides, such as the failure of public bidding on Mexico's high-speed train project since the end of 2014.

Mexico is probably one of the most extreme cases in the region of trade disparity with China, with an 11:1 import-export relationship. What little Chinese FDI has taken place in Mexico has specialized in manufacturing and services rather than the acquisition of raw materials as in most of Latin America and the Caribbean. The increasing disintegration of NAFTA, particularly in terms of trade between Mexico and the United States, is also evident in the continuously falling US share in Mexico's trade, from over 81 percent at the height of NAFTA (1999–2000) to below 65 percent since 2008; the US share in Mexican imports has fallen from 75 percent to less than 50 percent since 2007, affecting electronics, auto parts, automobiles, telecommunications, and other industries.

Recommendations

Mr. Chairman, I would invite the United States House of Representatives to consider the following actions:

1. Support, fund, and create public, academic, and private institutions in the United States to promote detailed understanding of and dialogue on the global reemergence of China, especially in Latin America and the Caribbean, since it also affects US trade, production, and employment, especially in manufacturing and automobiles and auto parts. Specifically support new "triangular" analysis and projects with concrete proposals regarding markets such as Latin America and the Caribbean, Mexico, and NAFTA in specific value-added chains such as telecommunications; electronics; yarn, textiles, and garments; and auto parts and automobiles.

2. Create institutions in the United States—in the Congress, Department of Commerce, and/or State Department—to discuss, together with Chinese and Latin American and Caribbean counterparts, the short-, medium-, and long-term implications of China's reemergence in the region and its socioeconomic, environmental, and labor sustainability.

3. Actively participate in and support the important work being done in Latin America and the Caribbean on the many issues related to this triangular relationship—such as statistics, trade, investment, tourism, visas, infrastructure, environment, and labor—by institutions such as CELAC, the Economic Commission for Latin America and the Caribbean, and the Inter-American Development Bank. This work is critical to a harmonious and sustainable triangular relationship. The elaboration of geostrategic and sector-related scenarios is also important. For example, the possibility of constructing a transoceanic canal in Nicaragua, funded by Chinese institutions and parallel to the

Panama Canal, could create new military, political, and socioeconomic challenges in the region and in its relationship with China and the United States.

China, in the last decade, has become the most dynamic socioeconomic and political partner of Latin America and the Caribbean; the United States has lost substantially in trade, investment, and financing terms, although its presence in Latin America and the Caribbean is still substantial and unquestioned. All three parties to this new triangular relationship will need to develop creative and vigorous strategies, policies, and instruments to meet the challenges arising from this new triangular relationship.

Thank you for your time. I look forward to your questions.

Mr. DUNCAN. Thank you very much for your testimony.

And the Chair will now recognize Ms. Joseph-Harris.

Thank you so much.

STATEMENT OF MS. SERENA JOSEPH–HARRIS, CHIEF EXECU-TIVE OFFICER, SIRIUS INTERNATIONAL (CARIBBEAN) DE-FENSE CONTRACTORS LTD. (FORMER HIGH COMMISSIONER OF THE REPUBLIC OF TRINIDAD AND TOBAGO)

Ms. JOSEPH-HARRIS. Thank you very much. And a very good evening to you, Chairman Duncan, Chairman Salmon, and Member Sires.

My contribution comes at a very——

Mr. DUNCAN. Could you pull that microphone down just a little bit? There you go.

Ms. JOSEPH-HARRIS. Is this better?

Mr. DUNCAN. There you go.

Ms. JOSEPH-HARRIS. Thank you very much.

My contribution comes at a very fortuitous time. It is the cul-mination of a 4-year inquisition that has just concluded in relation to the formidable strategic progress that China has been making in both hemispheres, so that the statement on hand will be con-fined to the following: I shall describe China's engagement with the Caribbean, why Caribbean countries are interested in Beijing, its objectives in the Caribbean and success to date, a description of the economic relations, and recommendations to the honorable Con-gress.

China is now the third-largest investor in the Caribbean, with the United States and the European Union occupying the two top spots. Its share of foreign investment regionally is an estimated 9 percent with trade volume of U.S., which is $156 billion.

Given this fairly modest quantum, in order to make sense of the region's magnetism to Beijing, we need to take stock of its strategic and ideological significance, bearing in mind that the Caribbean is part of the wider inter-American landscape, the history and char-acter of which is uniquely circumscribed by legal and political in-struments in principle and practice that has helped to shape this environment.

The PRC is, in contrast, unconversant with these aphorisms. If only for this reason, their engagements will have serious repercus-sions, potentially so, that can very well challenge the political cul-ture and democratic traditions and values of our hemisphere.

In order to understand Beijing's ambitions, we need to keyhole its interests. And these are essentially as follows in 11 short points: Sourcing and consolidating cheap supplies of food to sustain its burgeoning population.

Gaining comparative advantage along key trading routes. The Caribbean, as already alluded, takes the form of the port develop-ment projects, and it forms part of key chokepoints that are vital to Western Hemisphere trade and defense concerns.

Gaining access to raw materials and vital resources in anticipa-tion of the looming problem of a worldwide resource scarcity in fuels, metals, and minerals.

Infiltrating fuel markets through asset acquisition, as dem-onstrated in parts of the mainland, like Colombia and Venezuela.

Securing access to reserves of natural gas, which positions Trinidad and Tobago an ideal strategic partner.

Accessing and utilizing large areas of fertile land in promising locations, such as mainland Guyana, Suriname, and Belize.

Diversifying and consolidating its commercial portfolio to attain competitive advantage and market supremacy.

Introducing more enticing economic structures for countries to adopt. And this avenue provides a counterweight to the classical neoliberal model.

Gaining a foothold on the U.S. market indirectly through frontline jurisdiction, such as Bahamas and Jamaica.

And opening employment opportunities abroad for its tens of thousands of nationals that have been migrating to the urban areas in China in search of jobs.

I shall now get into the main areas in which the Caribbean has been more or less lured toward engaging with Beijing. These are the constraints that governments in the Caribbean have been constructed with, which causes them to look to Beijing and partner with it: Inflexible fiscal policies; low gross domestic product growth rates; high levels of violent crime and illicit traffic; the inability of our governments to attract development assistance; the increased liberalization of global trade, which has diminished market access; the small size of countries, which depletes from the full benefits of economies of scale; and the failure of intraregional single market arrangements; as well as the increasing costs of energy in the face of fluctuating prices.

Chairman, what I would recommend is that the U.S. and the Caribbean consolidate our deepening strategic relationships, which began in 2010 under the Caribbean Basin Security Initiative. This would essentially mean strengthening the regional security architecture through continued engagement with the United States, similar that has been done under the CBSI initiative, through more deepened security arrangements with our military, with our security and intelligence agencies, as well as interoperability and asset-sharing.

As a result of constraints of time, I would invite you, Chairman, and the rest of the listeners to refer to my most recently published inquisition, which provides compelling support in terms of statistical detail on those areas in which Beijing has been making inroads into the hemisphere. The study is called ''The Twilight of America's Omnipresence,'' and it gives an in-depth analysis of the military inroads, economic inroads, and political inroads being made by Beijing and makes suggestions as to how the United States could strengthen and build its relationship with the Caribbean in order to rebalance itself within the hemisphere.

Thank you, Chairman, for your time.

[The prepared statement of Ms. Joseph-Harris follows:]

CONGRESSIONAL TESTIMONY

Of

SERENA JOSEPH-HARRIS

Before the

SUBCOMMITTEE ON THE WESTERN HEMISPHERE

Of the

COMMITTEE ON FOREIGN RELATIONS

U.S. HOUSE OF REPRESENTATIVES

September 10, 2015

"China-Caribbean Economic and Trade Relations and Implications for the
United States – The Way Ahead"

Allow me first to thank the Chairman and Sub Committee members for the invitation to offer my testimony today on the subject of "China-Caribbean Economic and Trade Relations and Implications for the United States." I laud the efforts of the Subcommittee for holding this hearing and more so the timing of it. In recent weeks the media has been inundated with the responses of global markets to stock market jolts in Beijing as this resonated in both hemispheres.

Preamble

My contribution to this Subcommittee is a rejoinder to a trove of concerns which have been comprehensively anatomized in a recently concluded four-year inquisition that I had undertaken on the inroads made by the P.R.C. in the political, economic, diplomatic, technological and cultural spheres in the Americas and other hemispheres.

The Statement on hand is confined to the following themes -

- A description of China's engagement with the Caribbean.
- Why Caribbean countries are interested in Beijing and what Beijing's interests are in the Caribbean.
- China's objectives in the Caribbean and the success to date in achieving these objectives.
- A description of the economic relations between China and the Caribbean and the significance of these activities for U.S. interests (including positive and negative outcomes of Chinese engagements in the Caribbean) - this includes the areas of trade, purchase of assets and port transformation.
- Recommendations for the U.S. Congress on how to more effectively balance China's activities in the Caribbean.

Introduction

Chairman, we are well aware that the People's Republic of China (P.R.C.) is currently the world's second largest economy and in recent times its heightened interest in Caribbean economies has been a hotly debated topic among government officials, academia, defense planners and entrepreneurs. China is the most populous country in the world with an estimated 1.35 billion compared to 318.5 million in the United States and has accumulated a prodigious build-up of foreign reserves of which $1.5 billion is in US holdings. China has also surged ahead with alternative energies and continues to make impressive inroads in the sphere of innovation and technologies.

The P.R.C. has made its presence felt in the Caribbean and engagements so far are primarily economic. Less than one (1) percent of its trade with the world is conducted in the Caribbean. China is now the third largest investor in the Caribbean with the United States and the European Union occupying the top two spots. Its share of foreign investment regionally is an estimated 9% with a trade volume of US $ 156 billion. Given this modest quantum, in order to make sense of the region's magnetism to Beijing we need to take stock of its strategic and ideological significance, bearing in mind that the Caribbean is part of the wider Inter-American landscape the history and character of which is uniquely circumscribed by legal and political instruments that, in principle and in practice, have helped create an environment conducive to building and sustaining democratic institutions and the rule of law. The P.R.C. is in contrast unconversant with these aphorisms and if only for this reason their engagements will have repercussions that challenge the political culture of democratic tradition and values.

Another key consideration is that despite the existence of the OAS as the only credible and truly multilateral forum for political dialogue, our hemispheric institutional architecture is changing considerably. The last ten years has seen the the phenomenon of outward bound regionalism whereby the emergence of many subregional organizations such as ALBA, UNASUR and CELAC. These nascent multilateral blocs have highlighted the growing autonomy of the South thereby amplifying the need for strengthened, continuing and constructive dialogue. Added to this, the fall in the prices of commodities has precipitated a hemispheric economic downturn.

Concerns Among Analysts

Contacts between China and Latin America and the Caribbean are known to have existed and gone practically unnoticed for very many years. History would show that prior to the decline of a booming Asian market around 1800, there was a flourishing and interconnected world economy at the center of which China, as the Middle Kingdom, was very dominant. Apart from prodigious capital flows throughout East Asia typical of that period (1500-1800) there were equally significant flows of people and against this setting that Asian migratory movements to Latin America and the Caribbean (LAC) occurred in three discernible phases.

The first was during the pre-nineteenth century when the profitable three-century trade between Manila and Acapulco triggered an initial stream of migrations into Mexico and Peru. The second phase of migrants, commonly referred to as "the coolie trade" in Chinese Diaspora studies, was characteristic of the classic period between the nineteenth and twentieth centuries, renowned for the steady flow of indentured Chinese workers to the plantations of slave and former slave Americas, especially in relation to Cuba, Peru and to a lesser degree the British, French and Dutch Indies. Many Caribbean islands became the final destination of these arrivals, who constituted a distinct cohort from the prolonged influx of traders (huashang) that came before and thereafter. Commingled with the indentured migrants was a substantial number of persons that were literally "shanghaied," along with a less conspicuous group ignominiously labeled in relevant bills of lading as "cargo."

The more recent newcomers arrived in three further surges - initially out of the Guandung province in the early twentieth century; followed by a second stream from Hong Kong with the formation of the Republic in October 1949 following the defeat of the nationalist government by peasant-backed communists; with the most recent from the Fujian province during the 1980s and 1990s. Chinese triad activity permeated all migratory waves, and is known to have existed in many capitals of the region for well over one hundred years.

Defining the Caribbean

Chairman, for the purpose this Statement serves, the Caribbean would be taken to include: Anguilla (United Kingdom), Antigua and Barbuda, the Bahamas, the British Virgin islands (United Kingdom), Cayman Islands (United kingdom), Cuba, Curacao (Netherlands), Dominica, Dominican Republic, Grenada, Guyana, Haiti, Jamaica, Montserrat (United Kingdom), Navassa Island (United States), Puerto Rico (United States), St Barthelemy (France), St. Kitts and Nevis, St. Lucia, St. Martin (France), St. Vincent and the Grenadines, Sint Maarten (Netherlands), Trinidad and Tobago, Turks and Caicos Islands (United Kingdom), and the Virgin Islands (United States).

The region may be broadly divided into two groups: the first, which comprise the bulk of economies are largely dependent on tourism and offshore banking; and the second consists of a very small number of nations that are disproportionately dependent on mining, minerals and the agricultural commodity sectors. Regarding the former category, the IMF estimates that the tourism-based economies grew by only 1.1% in 2014 and are projected to expand by 1.7% in 2015. This notwithstanding, these countries are held back by numerous structural challenges that have constrained their economic performance and placed severe restrictions on avenues to promote profitable trade , commercial engagements and to access development financing.

What Beijing's Interests Are in the Caribbean

In order to get our arms around Beijing's interests in this part of the world we need to pay closer heed to how the Chinese policy evolved as well as to pertinent historical analogues. It would be recalled that roughly ten years ago China launched its China's Peaceful Development Road (2005). This was presented to the world in the form of a White Paper that completely and systematically clarified the Chinese government's theory and practice in its outreach to the developing world and its modernization agenda. It was a programmatic response articulating policy objectives specifically aimed at extending financial and development aid to developing and heavily indebted countries in various sub-regions. This represented Beijing's grand pitch for the stature of third world leader and regional power. No government worth its salt could resist such inducements, which in many instances, potentially set the stage for continued tenure of the political elite in many bankrupt countries.

Essentially the deal entailed (1) providing a zero tariff treatment for Least Developed Countries (LDC) with which China shared diplomatic relations; (2) expanding aid to Heavily Indebted Poor Countries (HIPC) and Least Developed Countries (LDC) through bilateral channels; (3) exempting or rescinding outstanding interest-free and low- interest loans due at the end of 2004 and owed by Heavily Indebted Poor Countries (HIPC) having diplomatic relations with China, within a two-year time frame; (4) financing $10 billion in preferential loans and preferential export buyers' credit to developing countries to help them upgrade their infrastructure within three years; (5) endorsing industrialization at bilateral level and conduct joint venture cooperation; and (6) increase aid to developing states in general. This road map and prescription was used to successfully infiltrate many African markets and its instructiveness lies in the striking analogies that can now be imputed in our hemispheric experiences.

The backdrop to this was that China saw the African continent as a venue of strategic opportunity given its natural resources including land space and promising demographic surge of 21st Century consumers. Latin America and the Caribbean hold out similar possibilities.

In addition to these economic incentives the Chinese Communist Party and top military strategists have moved in a clear-cut departure from conventional modeling. What this holds out for the Caribbean is the deployment of unconventional strategies that are perhaps unlooked for with tactfully applied soft power in the spheres of trade, financial, resource, cultural, technological and ecological means and which capitalize on the vulnerabilities of strategically important sectors of their respective societies. How leaders harness these strategic opportunities whilst retaining their commitment to the regional integration project - the commitment to which is incontestable - would require careful deliberation, intense collaboration and statecraft.

Beijing's strategy and objectives are being pursued by (1) exploiting the resource vulnerabilities of target nations' scarce or essential resources - ultimately this will place the P.R.C. in a position to control or deny the access and market value of critical commodities; (2) strategically positioning itself along key international shipping routes by investing in port facilities cheek by jowl with such routes; (3) launching or instigating non-kinetic assaults on financial systems to maintain economic high-ground over competitors and/or at worst flooding host markets with illegal goods; and (4) unleashing a concoction of ill-conceived media and cyber-warfare. These measures, which are by no mean untypical of the Chinese grand strategy, are being deployed through soft power rather than confrontationally, since to do otherwise would risk, and unnecessarily so, polarizing its most critical constituents in the region.

In order to put logic to Beijing's ambitions we need to keyhole its interests - which for the most part appear to be quite legitimate - and to recognize and how these converge with the disposition of the regional political elite to capitulate without hesitation to Chinese profligacy. What becomes patently clear judging from the PRC's historic course of conduct is that the CCP is placing its licensed focus on:

- Sourcing and consolidating cheap supplies of food to sustain its burgeoning population - China's population is 1,401,586,609 which is 19.13% of a world population of 7,324,782,225 (2015) with projected annual increases of 0.61% in 2015.
- Gaining comparative advantage in key trading routes - in the Caribbean, as already alluded, this takes the form of port development projects at key chokepoints which incidentally are vital to Western Hemisphere (American) trade and defense concerns.
- Gaining access to raw materials and vital resources in anticipation of the looming problem of worldwide resource scarcity in fuels, metals and minerals –in this regard, bauxite (aluminum ore) mining is a strong revenue source in countries like Suriname and this potential has been considerably bolstered by the discovery and exploitation of oil and gold; whilst Grenada in the southern Caribbean is a lead world producer of an array of spices including cinnamon, cloves and ginger mace.
- Infiltrating fuel markets through asset acquisition as demonstrated in projects in mainland Colombia, Venezuela and Ecuador.
- Securing access to reserves of natural gas which positions Trinidad and Tobago as an ideal strategic partner.
- Accessing and utilizing large areas of fertile land in promising locations such as mainland Guyana , Suriname and Belize.
- Diversifying and consolidating its commercial portfolio to attain competitor advantage and market supremacy while penetrating new markets and prevailing in already developed ones.
- Introducing more enticing economic structures for countries to adopt - this avenue provides a counterweight to the classic neoliberal model and its supporting Western monetary systems and carefully sidesteps conditionalities tied to democratic principles and universal rights.
- Gaining a foothold in the U.S. market indirectly through invigorated trade and investment initiatives in frontline jurisdictions, examples being the Bahamas and Jamaica.
- Opening employment opportunities abroad for its tens of thousands of nationals by negotiating large-scale infrastructural projects that effectively preclude the hiring of "host country" personnel - this helps to mitigate P.R.C. issues involving the mass migration of rural Chinese job-seekers to urban centers who are denied basic rights and are compelled to settle for low

wages, mandatory overtime, and dehumanizing living conditions; and the ever-present risk of mass civil unrest.

- Capitalizing on "game-changing transitions" and political vacuums. This was typified in the years immediately following the events of 9/11 with the drawdown of US interests in the Caribbean and America's re-direction of resources on the Middle East. Beijing seized upon this strategic opportunity to make impressive inroads into the Caribbean and Latin America in the fields of trade, investments, infrastructural development and military exchanges.
- Canvassing without let-up for the withdrawal of diplomatic support for Taiwan consistent with its "One-China" policy and concurrently building cordial relations with countries that recognize Taiwan, illustrated in its engagements with the Dominican Republic as a case in point.

Chairman, these strategic interests on China's part are valid. Indeed, they mirror Beijing's futuristic approach to planning and its deference to a rapidly evolving multipolar world with diverse opportunities and to equally formidable possibilities of vital resources drying up. Reciprocally, the political leaders of the Caribbean are concerned with their own domestic priorities and this brings us to the outcome of continuing Chinese overtures...and to the wider issue of to what extent they ultimately serve the interests of individual countries and the region as an integral limb of the Inter-American system.

Why Caribbean Countries Are Interested in Beijing

Chairman, the lure of Sino engagement becomes logical when one considers that the so-called "Golden Age of Latin America and the Caribbean" (2003-2013) has come to an end; that the region must now change gear to maintain what was achieved within the last decade; and that countries are now confronted with the fifth successive year of economic deceleration based on assessments of the World Bank (WB), the International Monetary Fund (IMF) and the Economic Commission for Latin America and the Caribbean (ECLAC). Caribbean countries are currently in the grips of structural economic constraints by which they are being crippled economically, politically and socially and see in China a world power replete with opportunities for monetary support through loans, trade, investments and funding; a feasible alternative to the U.S.A. and the EU for developmental aid and assistance; and a competent intermediary in terms of a voice for the global South that provides a buffer (when the need arises) in relations with the developed world.

Chairman, the key structural constraints facing the region can be directly attributed to diminishing trade and investment opportunities and this can be attributed to eight factors and I shall describe them as succinctly as possible, with your leave as time permits.

The constraints are: (1) inflexible fiscal policies (2) low gross domestic product growth (GDP) rates (3) high levels of violent crime and illicit traffic (4) their inability to attract development assistance (5) the increasing liberalization of global trade which has diminished market access (6) the small size of countries which depletes from the full benefits of economies of scale (7) the failure of intraregional single market arrangements to serve the interests of Caribbean Community members (8) the increasing costs of energy in the face of fluctuating prices.

(1) Inflexible Fiscal Policies

The first factor, the legacy of inflexible fiscal policies, has left many governments with little room for maneuver since the 2008 global financial crisis. The tourism destinations were particularly hard hit. In 2001, foreign visitors spent as much as 75% more per capita in the Caribbean than in broadly comparable destinations, and by 2010 this decided advantage had virtually disappeared. Equally material to this is that employment in most Caribbean countries is provided by the public sector whose unionized workers are often unwilling to support necessary changes advocated by policy makers.

(2) Low GDP Growth Rates

A second factor, the relatively low GDP growth rates of Caribbean economies, is attributed to the extraordinarily high levels of public debt amassed by these countries, as a percentage of their GDPs. Research has shown that Caribbean economies with GDP ratios above 56% suffer reduced economic growth due to the fact that investors refrain from making investments based on their expectations of lower returns and the possibility of higher taxes being imposed. As a case in point, the public debt of Barbados as a proportion of GDP continued to increase since 2012 from 84% that year to 103% in 2014; while in Jamaica the measure has remained above 130 % since 2009. In the meantime, St. Kitts and Nevis , Guyana and Jamaica continue to collaborate with the IMF to control their fiscal deficits. Nevertheless, despite these stout-hearted efforts the public debt in tourist-centered economies continues to exceed 90% of GDP on average and persists as a drag on sustainable growth.

(3) High Levels of Violent Crime

A third major drawback is the increasingly high levels of violent crime that has the potential to place at risk the performance of the hospitality sectors in already fragile economies, rendering then unattractive to investors.

(4)Inability to attract Development Asssistance

A fourth challenge resides the inability of countries to attract development assistance. This dilemma is owed to the status of many countries as upper middle or high-income societies. This somewhat misconceived categorization renders certain countries ineligible for development assistance with no guarantee of access to financial and other resources. Since the bulk of external finance in the Caribbean historically originates from Foreign Direct Investment (DFI) and remittances the key challenge confronting governments rests on firstly, devising ways of accessing capital for developmental concerns bearing in mind that private capital is driven by profit rather than by developmental needs; and secondly, in gaining access to alternative sources of finance since more traditional forms of financing for development, such as ODA, have declined ; and thirdly prevailing in a situation whereby in recent years donors that are no longer confined to member countries of the official Development Assistance Committee. This extended group of contributors has virtually mushroomed and is gaining in influence.

(5) Increasing liberalization of Global Trade

The fifth factor is the increasing liberalization of global trade and finance. This has eroded preferential access to developed country markets and increased the vulnerability of smaller markets to external market conditions.

(6) Smallness Diminishes Economies of Trade

A sixth consideration is that the small size of Caribbean economies limits their ability to attain full potential and reap the benefits of economies of scale and scope. Furthermore limited access to natural resources and labor supplies and high costs of transport, renders the cost of goods uncompetitive in the wider markets.

(7) CSME Has Fallen Short of Expectations

Chairman, one must also take into account developments in the trade arena at regional level, as well. The CARICOM Single Market and Economy (CSME) is an economic bloc among CARICOM countries established in 2006 to fulfill the objective of achieving a fundamental economic space. The rational for CSME was the sustained development of the standard of living of all Caribbean peoples through the Free Movement of Capital, Labor, Goods, the provision of services, the right of establishment with the Member States and the establishment of a common external tariff. However, the mechanism has registered a disappointing track record due to the underperformance of intraregional trade and the disproportionate advantage it affords to larger members to the detriment of the smaller partners.

(8) Increasing Costs of Energy and Fluctuating Prices

As in all regions of the world, the cost of energy is a critical factor more so for non-oil producing countries. The recent economic and political developments in Venezuela could put at risk the benefits that are currently available through the mechanism of Petrocaribe. One of the advantages of this compact is that up to 50% of all oil purchases can be converted into 25 year loans at interests rates from as low as 1%. A tenor of optimism resonated on the eve of the 10th Commemorative

Summit of the Petrocaribe Agreement hosted by the Jamaican government when the it was hinted that upon the conclusion of the annual devaluation of the Agreement, there would be set in motion among signatories to strengthen and deepen the Agreement by pursuing expanded opportunities, one being the issue of regional transportation.

Chairman, you would no doubt appreciate the complexity of coordinating and combining a wide cross-section of actors, funding mechanisms and instruments under a coherent development financing architecture that is favorable to the region. This lack of coherence at national and regional levels has opened up "opportunities" for the P.R.C.

I shall now briefly advert to the region's trade portfolio vis-à-vis China. There is a progressively widening trade deficit in the Caribbean that works overwhelmingly in China's favor. This is due to the nature of goods being traded. The main products imported from China into the region consist of ships, boats and other floating structures; machinery nuclear reactors and boilers; iron and steel; plastics; articles of apparel; prefabricated buildings; footwear and the like; whilst Caribbean exports consist in large part of raw materials, inorganic chemicals; precious metal compounds, iron and steel, mineral fuels, oil and distillation products, aluminum, slag and ash. In 2012 Jamaica's Prime Minster the Honorable Portia Simpson-Miller, while reiterating her commitment to regionalism, observed that the trade imbalances with China were in fact a distorting feature in the fifteen-member trade bloc.

A Description of China's Engagements with the Caribbean

Chairman, the Third China Caribbean Trade and Economic Forum was a major milestone for the region since it precipitated an open-handed flow of loan and concessional arrangements between the PRC and many governments. That year a loan agreement valued at $400,000 million for infrastructural work on the Montego Bay Convention Center was signed by the Jamaican government along with a further $600,000 million loan agreement for infrastructural work and the $65.3 Million Palisadoes Peninsula project negotiated with the China EXIM Bank. Equally notable, the Chinese company COMPLANT acquired the assets of Jamaica's sugar industry to invest in the renovation of three of the country's sugar factories and lands (Douglas 2011).

At the said forum, Trinidad and Tobago received 40 million Yuan in grant funding from the Chinese government. This gesture was preceded by a concessional loan for the construction of a National Academy of the Performing Arts (NAPA) and an additional 210 million Yuan in concessional loans for completion of infrastructural work on the facility in March 2011 (Tach 2010). A Chinese corporation, Investment Corporation (CIC), initiated the acquisition of ten percent stake from the French firm GDF Suez in Atlantic LNG in Trinidad and Tobago. The Chinese have also committed to funding a Children' Hospital in Trinidad. Not to be outdone, a Technical Agreement was signed between the Chinese and Bahamian governments ahead of the 2009 China Caribbean Trade and Economic Forum freeing up funding for infrastructural projects and bringing total Chinese investments in that country to a whopping $2.66 billion by 2011 (Thomson 2011).

Barbados was also well endowed. The Chinese agreed to provide Barbados with a grant of roughly BDS $6.15 million to underwrite an array of small-scale development projects (Greene 2011); and a further Chinese grant would fund four score boards for the renowned Widley Gymnasim, the country's premier indoor sports facility, valued at BBS $3.38 million (Austin 2011). Guyana has in turn benefitted from a trove of grants, interest free and concessional loans and the writing off of no less than nine (9) mature debts.

As well, the Commonwealth of Dominica is venue to a series of infrastructural projects coming on stream after receiving a ECD $7.2 million endowment under a Technical and Economic Cooperation Agreement (2007). The negotiated agreement involved grant aid of US $100,000.00 for disaster relief in that country (Government of Dominica 2007). Antigua and Barbuda also received concessionary loans and grants. These went towards the construction of the Sir Vivian Richards Cricket Stadium, an airport terminal and a secondary school in Five Islands (Caribarena News 2011); whilst eighty-six (86) percent of the cost of rehabilitating the regionally acclaimed St. Paul's Sports, Cultural and Development Organization in Grenada was provided by the PRC.

This is a mere snapshot of the wider panorama of economic engagements between Caribbean countries and the P.R.C.

Assessment of China's Objectives and Success and Intra-Regional Dynamics

U.S. Debt Held by China

Chairman, the elephant in the room is irrefutably the US $1.261 Trillion debt held by China as the United States' largest foreign creditor, only second to Japan's share of debt held, which according to US Treasury data, amounted to US $1.227 Trillion in February 2015. In order to stimulate demands for Chinese goods, Beijing has been keeping its money cheap by maintaining a low value for the remnibi and simultaneously buying up U.S. dollars. China thus becomes a major player in sustaining confidence in the US dollar over the short-term and bolstering its survivability in the longer-term. In divergence to this, Beijing's responses resonate many versions of assault ranging from suggestions to trade partners to abandon trading in U.S. currency, to engaging in "money swaps" as what transpired with Argentina in 2009, employing gold as an international reference point, introducing the notion of a new global currency as it did in the BRICS Summits of 2009 and

2012, diversifying its cash reserves away from dollar determined instruments of any kind, and the indiscriminate purchasing of gold. Currency wars, as we are all aware, are among the most deadly non-kinetic weapons that can be unleashed on a country and they have the potential to disrupt the world's financial systems in a serious way. Any shift from the U.S. dollar as the reserve currency is therefore worthy of attention.

Posthaste, Beijing has now moved to introduce remnibi in its trade relations with CARICOM. This was formalized with signing of an agreement in principle in 2015 between the PRC and the Bahamas and paves the way for trade using remnibi currency. In 2013, the World Bank ranked the Bahamas as one of the wealthiest nations in the Caribbean Community based on its prolific offshore banking centers. This agreement therefore opens up a range of benefits and opportunities for both signatories including currency exchange savings from direct bilateral transactions ; same-day or expedited currency exchanges for time-sensitive transactions; the strengthening of trade and investment relationship between signatories; and notably the possibility of extending remnibi settlement services to other Caribbean partners. It also becomes crystal clear that asymmetric linkages are being tactfully crafted, much to the credit of Chinese diplomatic aplomb, and this is not necessarily confined to trade and finance, as shall be demonstrated.

Port Infrastructure

Chairman, it is history that from the late nineties, Beijing has made impressive in-roads in port infrastructural development and this brand of entrepreneurialism has consistently found its way to locations that constitute crucial hemispheric chokepoints. Amidst the ongoing discourse among defense analysts are hints of a possible threat that this may pose to Western trade and the U.S. defense posture. However, such undertones can be readily dispelled from an economic standpoint, since given the emergence of new trade partnerships, it is conceivable that China is positioning itself for securing high-ground in a growing Asian market as Asia re-asserts itself and assumes center-stage in the global economy.

i.   For starters in the Bahamas the Hong-Kong-based Hutchinson Whampoa Limited shipping giant is responsible for what is arguably the largest Chinese investment in that country and has been in operation since 1997. The company is owned by Hong Kong tycoon Li Ka-Shiing, who has personal ties to the People's Liberation Army (PLA). Estimated at US $2.6 Billion, the hub occupies a whopping 88 acres of the 530 square mile land space of the Grand Bahamas Island and enjoys 3,400 feet of berthing and a projected annual capacity of 1 million 20-foot equivalent units (TEU).

ii. The Panama Canal is another of the better-known examples of Sino port diplomacy. Located a mere 900 miles from the U.S. and controlling at least one third of the world's shipping, the canal is vital to Western trade and defense. 20% of US imports and exports pass through the Canal along with 40% of all grain exports. A Chinese corporation called the Great Wall of Panama has a 60 year lease for an export zone at the Atlantic end of the Canal. Hutchinsom Whampoa, the Hong Kong-based multinational conglomerate with a market capitalization of roughly US $53 Billion, has already ploughed in excess of US $100,00,000 to manage Port Cristobal on the Atlantic end and Port Balboa on the Pacific side. Moreover, the conglomerate is 10% owned by China Reserves Enterprises (CRE) which is reputedly a front-base for Chinese military intelligence. I need say no more.

iii. The Nicaragua Canal and Development Project is the most recent demonstration of Chinese strategic posture in an obvious attempt to eclipse the Panama Canal and possibly stage-manage a major shipping route that would connect the Caribbean Sea to the Pacific Ocean. In June 2013, Nicaragua's General Assembly approved a Bill to grant a 50 year concession to a private corporation , the Hong Kong Nicaragua Canal Development Company (HKND), headed by Chinese billionaire Wang Jing. At one point Russia had expressed an interest in this venture. However as of August 2015 no significant development has taken place. It is noteworthy that the terms of reference of this deal confer on the HKND group, "...the sole rights ...to plan, design, construct and thereafter to operate and manage the Nicaragua Grand Canal and other related projects including ports , a free trade zone, an international airport and other infrastructural development projects..."

Taken in tandem these highly visible port projects and others on the mainland in places like Colombia, Peru, Chile, Ecuador and Mexico are making the region more connected and accessible and serve as a prognostication of much awaited expanded commerce between the Caribbean and Latin America and booming Asian markets . The region's strategic geography in combination with China's market-oriented approaches have undoubtedly provided a boon in making this possible.

The Taiwan Issue

Intra-regional dynamics is also visible in the sphere of an Asian policy. The failure within CARICOM to arrive at a consensus on the China-Taiwan issue works to the detriment of the region by amplifying divided loyalties and shifting priorities at Community and local levels. Of the fifteen members of CARICOM, four currently have diplomatic relations with Taiwan while eleven maintain diplomatic ties with the P.R.C. At Community level, under the Revised treaty of Chaguaramas that establishes CARICOM, signatories of the 15 member bloc commit to "enhanced coordination of member states' foreign and (foreign) economic policies." Despite this there is ambivalence surrounding the issue at subregional levels primarily among the Organization of Eastern Caribbean States (OECS) which comprises six independent countries. So that despite the obligations of signatories under two treaties, in the case of CARICOM to "harmonize" foreign policy; and in the case of the OECS compact to "coordinate" their foreign policy , neither the letter nor the spirit is upheld in the China-Taiwan issue and this has delayed the formulation of a cohesive policy towards Asia.

Once again, Beijing's largesse fostered by the Chinese Communist Party (CCP), state-backed banks and pro-establishment corporations appears to have created fissures in the region that go beyond the incentivization of governments to precipitating spirited competition that erodes attempts for more coordinated approaches to trade and economic foreign relations.

Furthermore, a closer scrutiny of bilateral trade arrangements discloses that Chinese trade and investment agreements with Caribbean countries restrict knowledge and technology transfer, and in lieu of this, insist upon the hiring of Chinese nationals as a pre-condition. Invariably, this restriction works to the disadvantage of the local employment market and breeds disaffection among nationals, often drawing heated protests, as obtained in the Bahamas and Guyana, which are by no means singular examples.

Assessment and Recommendations

Proximity, vulnerability and instability have made the Caribbean Basin of particular strategic interest to the United States and it is primarily for this reason the U.S. Congress has approved an array of trade preference programs. The economic and political stability of the Caribbean is vital to U.S. security interests and trade relations and this was the underpinning factor in the Monroe Doctrine which is motivated by commercial, political and security interests. Against this setting unilateral trade preferences became integral to the U.S. foreign economic policy. These types of trade arrangements give market access to selected developing country goods, duty free or at tariffs below normal rates, without requiring reciprocal trade concessions. These arrangements have taken many forms with the common goal of promoting economic growth and development in poor and developing countries.

As I have previously iterated, attention must now be directed to the wider financial landscape where changes have led to increasing complexities for the region regarding how to combine financing options under a coordinated architecture in an environment in which domestic resource mobilization must be treated as a key pillar for development. Let us therefore consider some of the principal trade preferences that have been implemented in U.S-Caribbean trade relations, what lessons can be learnt from them and how this could inform future trade arrangements between the United States and the Caribbean.

Chairman , I wish to recall that in 1964 the U.S. government ushered in the preferential tariff program based on production sharing. The Caribbean Basin and Mexico were early beneficiaries of this agreement whose major advantage was in production sharing based on a mutually competitive business strategy, proximity, and low transportation costs. By the 1970s there was a shift in policy to preference programs, that is to say, unilateral trade preferences as a form of development assistance. This materialized with the Generalized System of Preferences (GSP) under the auspices of the General Agreement on Tariffs and Trade (GATT)which permitted developed countries to grant unilateral tariff preferences for selected imports for developing countries. The U.S. GSP Program which was, as previously alluded, driven by regional security needs, required Congressional approval and was last authorized through December 31, 2010.

In the early eighties concerns over the region's economic collapse and political radicalization resulted in attempts to usher in the Caribbean Basin Initiative (CBI) . Two points on this score must be made clear: the first is that the first bill of the CBI died in the 97th Congress due to objections raised by interests representing import competing firms to the proposed tax incentives, aid and trade preferences; the second is that the unpopularity of the Bill prompted the passage of the Caribbean Basin Economic Recoveries Act (CBERA 1983) which, like its precursor, drew stiff resistance from U.S. textile and labor interests and ultimately had to be radically scaled back to modest duty-free treatment for a mere 10 percent of Caribbean exports. Twenty-seven countries, including members of the CARICOM bloc, were beneficiaries of this pact. All were eligible for duty-free or reduced duty access for selected exports, provided that they satisfied specific U.S. requirements. This, Chairman, is a significant criterion given the non-doctrinaire posture attributed by the Chinese to related deals. Countries designated by Washington as "Communist countries;" those which had seized U.S. properties without compensation; nations that failed to recognize or enforce awards arbitrated in favor of U.S. citizens; those that afforded preferential treatment to goods from other countries to the detriment to U.S. commerce; broadcasted U.S. copyright material without permission; had not signed an extradition agreement with the United States; or had not taken steps to afford internationally recognized worker rights were automatically disentitled to benefitting from the program. A further caveat lay in exceptions imposed for specific articles defined by the Congress as "import sensitive." These included textile and apparel articles under the Multi Fiber Arrangement, petroleum products, footwear, handbags, luggage, flat goods, work gloves, leather wearing apparel, canned tuna, and watches or watch parts.

The Caribbean call for the inclusion of a greater number of Caribbean goods to qualify for additional tariff benefits to textiles, apparel, sugar, petroleum and leather goods and other items excluded from the 1983 legislation and appeals for CBERA to become a permanent program, did not go unheeded. This would find its way into amended legislation in which textiles and apparels were again removed making way for the passage instead of Title II of the Customs and Trade Act; tariff granted tariffs for certain items like handbags, luggage, flat goods, work gloves and leather goods and would be phased in over time ; reduced tariffs for items that eligible for GPS treatment; and fresh wave of limited benefits for ethanol products .

CBI, which had provided preferential entry into the United States for the majority of Caribbean exports was eventually eroded with the ushering in of NAFTA, the most glaring example being in the area of apparel exports . NAFTA provided to Mexico duty and quota free access for textile and apparel products in excess of that which was accorded to the Caribbean. This resulted in a situation in which Mexican apparel exports were growing at a rate three times that of the Caribbean. The Caribbean Textile Apparel Institute estimated that NAFTA had been a factor in the loss of roughly 123,000 jobs in the region and the closure of no less than 150 apparel factories. The situation was compounded by the challenge to the EU banana regime launched by a U.S –led coalition of Latin American countries. This second course of action precipitated the dismantlement of the banana industry in the Windward Islands, which accounted at time, for an estimated 16.5 percent of the GDP and 40 to 80 percent of total export earnings.

The Haitian Hemispheric Opportunity Through Partnership Encouragement Act of 2006(HOPE I) which was intended to introduce new trade preferences for Haiti also warrants special mention. This agreement was sui generis based on the fact that the United States is the main destination for Haitian apparel exports which comprise the country's dominant export sector, generating an estimated 80% of its foreign exchange. Added to this, the apparel sector provides a potential avenue for employment growth. With these concerns in view, HOPE I permits the duty free treatment for apparel imports in limited quantities assembled, knit-to-shape in Haiti with inputs from third-part countries, and countries outside the region that are not party to either a preferential trade arrangement or free trade arrangement with the United States. Taking all things into account, Congress amended the CBERA at its 109th.Session with the passage of HOPE I. The revised legislation provided enhanced benefits for Haitian goods in the form of duty- free treatment for select apparel imports made in part from a less expensive country, and yarns and fabrics provided that Haiti met the eligibility criteria relating to core labor rights, human rights and anti-poverty policies.

In order to ensure the full realization of HOPE I, HOPE II was introduced with the specific aim of making the rules and Regulations under the Food, Conservation and Energy Act of 2008 simpler and more flexible. HOPE II required Haiti to create a new apparel sector monitoring program and labor Ombudsman to ensure that country' compliance with internationally recognized core labor principles. Thereafter and following the earthquake in 2010, Congress enacted the Haiti Economic Lift Program (HELP) by amending the HOPE Act to provide for more free-handed trade preferences aimed at encouraging increased investment in the country's apparel assembly businesses that would ultimately contribute to increases in output, exports and employment.

Another more recent shift in the U.S.-led trade preference landscape occurred when the Dominican Republic Central America United States Free trade Agreement

(CAFTA-DR) was launched on March 01, 2006. This agreement has resulted in nearly full free trade between the U.S. and partner countries once fully implemented. Provisions covering textile and apparel , the largest import category for the region, were made permanent and provided that components are sourced from any one of the member countries the finished assembled product can be exported to the United States, duty free.

This review is by no means exhaustive but provides a fair snapshot of policies pursued by the U.S. to promote more diversified and multi-track trade preference programs and free trade agreements in its efforts to increase imports from partners in the hemisphere. It also demonstrates the fact that there is a viable and reciprocal trade relationship between the United States and regional partners based on reciprocity and that from time to time positions must be negotiated based on converging an diverging interests.

Chairman, U.S. policies are logically driven by U.S. interests in much the same way as China's policies are driven by Chinese interests. The Caribbean in turn has to charter a course for itself to achieve a win-win.

Recommendations on How to Rebalance

It is obvious that since the 1990s, trade integration has resulted in cooperation among Latin American and Caribbean partners and that many countries have pursued a multi-tiered liberalization strategy comprising a combination of unilateral opening; regional trade agreements inclusive of free trade arrangements ; customs unions exemplified among our MERCOSUR partners further south; common markets; and multilateral trade liberalization under the WTO. But this has not adequately supported the interests of the smaller countries. Neither have sub-regional integration initiatives – among which is the Caribbean Single market and Economy - achieved the set goals.

Pragmatic alternatives must now be considered: consolidating trade preferences and moving towards deeper common markets is one option. Another is devising politically feasible solutions in response to the proliferation of preferential trade Agreements in the form of "convergence" – a process by which regional Free Trade Areas could become connected to each other with tariff elimination being a pre-condition.

However, China is ubiquitous to this debate given its impressive market penetration into critical strategic areas and the fact that the P.R.C. now has to protect and consolidate its investments. To compound this, the lack of adequate physical infrastructure and less than robust trade links in the Caribbean (and to a large extent Latin America) precludes closer integration. This contrasts with Asia's engine growth which is largely fuelled by robust infrastructure and a complex network of vertical supply chains that contribute to intra-firm and intra-industry trade and integrated cross-supply chains - these very assets that are foundational for 21st

Century sustainable development in the region. China recognizes this and has adopted a futuristic outlook, positioning itself for a multipolar world in which Asia would assume preeminence, economically speaking. Here is where the Caribbean-Pacific gateway becomes crucial.

A Congressional Research Paper entitled "U.S. Trade Policy and the Caribbean: From Trade Preferences to Free trade Agreements" produced in January 2011 by J.J. Hornbeck, Specialist in International Trade and Finance, anatomizes successive U.S. trade agreements and policy options that can inform the way ahead , when the "design flaws" of tariff preference programs of the past are taken into account. Admitting that structural design flaws in Caribbean tariff preference programs can limit the effectiveness of unilateral trade, Hornbeck believes that given the proliferation of large low-cost Asian producers and the increasing substitution by the United States of the reciprocal Free Trade Agreements the strategy of selective export and economic growth may have run its full course. Three options on the way ahead were raised.

The first option was to allow the trade preference programs to expire - was rejected previously rejected by Congress on grounds that such course of action is likely to trigger a potential bi-lateral FTA. The second was to redefine the unilateral preference programs – raises another range of concerns. The argument was that except for energy and chemical exports which comprise just short of 80% of CARICOM's merchandize exports to the U.S. , barring the CAFTA-DR the remaining CBI countries will have little to take advantage of. It is unlikely that Caribbean countries could benefit considerably under apparel goods which currently amount to less than 5% of CBI exports. The third was a possible U.S. – CARICOM FTA.

Key to all of this is that CARICOM nations have a large service sector, with a focus on tourism, financial and professional services. As already discussed, labor costs and the cost of transportation and energy erode competitiveness. This is a given. Hence, a U.S. market for goods emanating out of CARICOM becomes less incentivized. Another critical concern is the diversity and disparity between countries with the most vulnerable smaller countries disposed to reticence in renegotiating; the more developed countries like Trinidad and Tobago more amenable to an FTA, but less so than natural resource-based countries like Guyana and Jamaica.

The Caribbean Basin Security Initiative

In light of the above, my view is that at this critical point in time the U.S. could exploit its already deepened security relationships with the Caribbean which are rooted in Inter-American idealism, common concerns and a rich history of interoperability among our security forces and agencies . Given the shifting priorities of regional leaders, prevailing economic disparities, a situation of outward bound regionalisms whereby countries are members of overlapping blocs (not all of which share the same ideological persuasions) compounded by the slowing down of the U.S. economy, the most feasible option would appear to be for us to "close ranks" and recalibrate and consolidate those efforts that are grounded in common concerns such as transborder criminality as a case in point.

Members of this House may recall that in 2010 the Caribbean Basin Security Initiative (CBSI) was launched at a time when Caribbean societies were reeling under an unprecedented surge in gun-related murders and violence and renewed waves in the illicit drugs and firearms trade. The initiative was part of wider hemispheric responses to increase public safety and security and promote social justice. An initial appropriation of US $43 million was allocated to the program in 2010 to be increased to $79 million in the following year. At a Round Table hosted by the Institute of National Strategic Studies (INSS) in Spring of 2010 precursory to the CBSI launch to discuss ways and means of enhancing North South dialogue, I called attention to the need for programmatic responses that were aligned with the concerns of regional governments noting, among other things, that -

"A US conceived region-wide strategy that aims at responding should ideally be complementary to the security concerns of regional governments."

The Alpha Barrier of North South Dialogue (2010)

These views were shared with the U.S. Ambassador in Port of Spain in 2011. I recognized at that time, and still do, that security is indispensable to development and sustainable economic growth and equally vital to preserving peace and security and the attainment of good governance. In fact, none of these is mutually exclusive. This call is in alignment with President Obama's undertaking at the Fifth Summit of the Americas hosted in Port of Spain, Trinidad in 2009 for *a new era of engagement* to achieve prosperity throughout the Americas and imputed a reframing of the discourse. CBSI committed to deepening security cooperation in the Caribbean and the cooperative dialogue process in order to sustain capabilities in (1) maritime and aerial security cooperation (2) law enforcement and capacity building (3) justice sector reform and (4) citizen security as a social dimension. However, we need to enlarge now upon CBSI's goals and achievements which are essentials to economic recovery – this is every government's top priority.

First: my appeal is for partners to recommit to the elementals of the Inter-American Democratic Charter - respect for the rule of law; human rights and fundamental freedoms; periodic free and fair elections; a pluralistc system of political parties; the separation and independence of powers and fundamental core values and values such as probity and transparency in governance. This is well in train. Then we adopt a programmatic approach to CBSI with focus placed on institutional strengthening of the regional security architecture while simultaneously building capacity at satellite bodies in each capital thereby preserving the legacy of Cricket World Cup which should not be allowed to go astray.

Reconsolidating this partnership would be a timely move in light of recent changes on the political landscape of Guyana and Trinidad and Tobago – which along with other partners provided the impetus and commitment for this effort. Of this we are assured.

Chairman, let me once more applaud the efforts of this Committee and record my appreciation for the opportunity to contribute my views and recommendations. I have the fullest confidence in the potential of a reinvigorated Caribbean-U.S. partnership under the umbrella of a revamped CBSI. May God continue to favor your arduous and unstinting efforts.

Thank you very much.

Mr. DUNCAN. I want to thank you.

And now Ms. Myers is recognized for 5 minutes.

Thank you.

STATEMENT OF MS. MARGARET MYERS, PROGRAM DIRECTOR, CHINA AND LATIN AMERICA, INTER–AMERICAN DIALOGUE

Ms. MYERS. Thank you, and good afternoon. I would like to thank the committee and subcommittee chairmen and ranking members and other esteemed committee members for the opportunity to be here today. I will be summarizing my written testimony, which I have submitted for the record.

Let me begin by saying that this hearing, ''China's Advance in Latin America and the Caribbean,'' is very appropriately titled. As we have discussed, China's presence in Latin America and other regions has grown at a remarkable rate in just over a decade.

Latin American and Caribbean exports to China have increased 23 percent per year, on average, since 2000, although that has slowed rather considerably in recent years. We have talked a lot about the $119 billion in finance that China has given to Latin America since 2005, and most of that is going to Venezuela, Ecuador, Argentina, and Brazil. There are numerous investors now present in Latin America—small private ones, large SOEs, banks, both commercial and policy banks, and also China's sovereign wealth fund, although China's foreign direct investment in the region is still fairly low.

China's growing presence, as we have mentioned, in Latin America is also apparent in cultural, educational, military, and political spheres, although over the past decade and a half so much of overall engagement has supported the objectives of China's so-called ''going out'' strategy. And these include securing access to raw materials, establishing new markets for Chinese exports, promoting Chinese brands—and there are many, many Chinese brands in Latin America now—and internationalizing Chinese firms.

And much of what we see China doing in the region today can still be viewed as supporting these objectives. In this sense, China's interest in the region has been rather static. But the relationship has also evolved in some very important ways, and I would like to use my remaining time to briefly highlight three examples.

We have, first of all, seen some important changes in the way in which Chinese firms are investing in the region. Especially in the agriculture and energy sectors, there are growing efforts to invest not only in crop cultivation and mining and drilling, for example, but across entire supply chains—in production, processing, logistics, and marketing—this in order to better control supply and pricing and also to compete with other multinationals and also U.S. firms.

Like in Asia, Latin America has also seen growing interest from China in the development of cross-regional transportation infrastructure, such as the proposed Brazil-Peru railway, but there are many, many other examples. These projects are largely intended to facilitate the transport of raw materials to port, especially along the Pacific coast. Pacific maritime routes are often favorable to those that go through the Gulf of Aden or other areas—transport security, in other words.

Second, there is a perceived change or a growing focus on the part of China in region-wide diplomatic initiatives in Latin America and the Caribbean. And we have mentioned already the China-CELAC forum, which was established in 2014 and which excludes the U.S. and Canada. China has also recently announced several new regional credit lines and investment funds. China's central bank announced this month that it will establish a $10 billion fund for investment in Latin American manufacturing or production capacity.

And, finally, we have seen some important changes in Chinese firm operations. Recent case study analysis suggests that Chinese companies have made real advances in community relations and adherence to local, environmental, and labor standards. But complaints about Chinese companies continue to surface, and the environmental standards of China's top lenders to Latin America are still weaker than those of other international financial institutions. There are also indications, troubling indications, that some Latin American governments have intentionally weakened standards and regulations in order to attract Chinese and other investment or to facilitate cross-Pacific trade.

And China's ongoing financial support for certain governments in the region, to include Maduro in Venezuela, is thought to enable continued economic mismanagement and to facilitate corruption and standards erosion.

So I would conclude simply by saying that China is and will continue to be an important economic partner for many countries in the region, even as economic growth slows on both sides of the Pacific. Whether China-Latin America relations are, in fact, a win-win and mutually beneficial, as China indicates, is debatable. Chinese economic engagement has certainly contributed to growth in some countries in the region, and Chinese investment could be helpful for some Latin American industries or sectors. But mutual benefit requires the regions' governments to negotiate effectively and maintain necessary environmental, labor, and other standards. And I think that the U.S. has a real role in potentially facilitating these developments.

Thank you very much.

[The prepared statement of Ms. Myers follows:]

HEARING BEFORE THE
HOUSE COMMITTEE ON FOREIGN AFFAIRS

China's Advance in Latin America and the Caribbean

September 10, 2015

Margaret Myers
Director, China and Latin America Program
Inter-American Dialogue

I would like to thank the Committee and Subcommittee Chairmen and Ranking Members and the other esteemed committee members for the opportunity to be here today.

Let me begin by saying that this hearing is very appropriately titled. China's presence in Latin America and the Caribbean (LAC) – and other regions of the world, for that matter – has grown at a remarkable rate in just over a decade. Latin American and Caribbean exports have increased 23 percent per year on average since 2000. And Chinese banks have provided approximately $119 billion in finance to the region since 2005. An increasingly wide variety of investors – e.g., private Chinese companies (large and small), state-owned enterprises, Chinese policy and commercial banks, and China's sovereign wealth fund – are evident in the region.

China's growing presence in LAC is also apparent in the cultural, educational, military, and political spheres. Technical and military cooperation and ministerial dialogue are features of the relationship in many countries. In the academic realm, China is actively cooperating with Asian studies centers in Latin American universities and by financing Confucius Institutes across the region.

A Rapidly Evolving Relationship

As the China-Latin America relationship grows, it is also evolving. China's approach to LAC has changed in the past few years – the result of numerous factors, including changing economic conditions in both China and Latin America, shifting patterns of consumption in China, the internationalization and professionalization of Chinese firms, and China's evolving strategic considerations.

The following are three examples of recent shifts in Chinese engagement with LAC:

1. *Chinese companies are exploring new approaches to investment in LAC and other regions.*

For almost two decades, China has pursued fairly static "going-out" objectives in LAC. These include securing access to raw materials, establishing new markets for Chinese exports, promoting Chinese brands, and internationalizing Chinese firms.

Much (though not all) of what China is doing in LAC today still supports Beijing's "going-out" goals. Chinese trade with and foreign direct investment in the region are still overwhelmingly focused on the acquisition of raw materials and agricultural goods. Chinese companies also continue to seek new markets for increasingly high-tech exports. And Chinese brands, such as Lifa, Lenovo, Huawei, and Haier, are increasingly popular among the region's consumers.

But China's approach to achieving these objectives has changed over time. This is especially evident in terms of investment.

Having learned from the 2007-8 global food crisis, for example, China's agricultural giants have adopted new overseas investment strategies. No longer content to rely solely on international traders for agricultural supply from Latin America, COFCO, China's top grains trader, is planning to invest across the agricultural supply chain (in production, processing, logistics, and marketing) to better control food supply and pricing.

Mergers and acquisitions (M&A) are also becoming increasingly prevalent as China seeks access to key markets/resources and "know-how" from local firms and multinationals with years of experience in the region. Chinese oil company, Sinopec, acquired a 30 percent stake in Galp Energia Brazil in 2011. And Brazilian oil firm, Petrobras, sold its Peruvian subsidiary to China National Petroleum Company (CNPC) for $2.6 billion in 2013. Backed by US$10 billion from China Development Bank and Agricultural Bank of China, COFCO has recently begun acquiring firms (e.g., Nidera and Noble Group) with assets across the region.

Chinese companies are also increasingly partnering with foreign firms in overseas deals. Mexican and Chinese firms jointly bid on a high-speed passenger rail project in Mexico, for example, although that deal eventually collapsed. In the region's mining and energy sectors, Chinese companies are increasingly taking stakes in consortia instead of seeking 100 percent control over an asset. Chinese oil companies, CNPC and China National Offshore Oil Corporation, each have a 10 percent stake in Brazil's offshore Libra oil field. Chinese companies are also working with local legal and marketing firms in an effort to navigate host-country regulations and markets.

Also apparent is growing interest in the development of cross-regional transportation infrastructure, such as the proposed Brazil-Peru railway and a bi-oceanic Chilean tunnel. These projects support multiple objectives, but are largely intended to facilitate the transport of raw materials to ports, especially along the Pacific Coast. The China-backed renovation of Argentina's Belgrano-Cargas railway could promote transport of Argentine soy to the Chilean border and then to port, for example.

In addition to supporting resource acquisition, infrastructure proposals and new Latin America-focused investment policies also support elements of China's economic reform agenda. Large overseas rail projects are thought to address overcapacity in China's steel industry. China's newly-announced "1+3+6" and "3x3" frameworks for cooperation with

Latin America promote economic upgrading by encouraging greater involvement of China's private and public companies in high-tech and manufacturing sectors in Latin America, such as telecommunications, logistics, rail, and shipbuilding.

2. *Chinese is growing its diplomatic presence in LAC.*

If it ever was, China is no longer tip-toeing around the U.S. when engaging LAC. As in Africa and Asia, China has made major diplo-economic strides in the region in past two years alone.

China engages not only left-leaning, centrally-run governments, but nearly every country in Latin America and the Caribbean, including the market-oriented Pacific Alliance nations. Li Keqiang discussed infrastructure investment in Colombia and Peru and planned a currency swap with Chile during his May 2015 trip to the region.

In addition to maintaining an active presence in several regional organizations (e.g., the Organization of American States and the Inter-American Development Bank), China and the Community of Latin American and Caribbean States (CELAC, which excludes the U.S. and Canada) established a new forum in 2014, during President Xi Jinping's visit to Fortaleza, Brazil. The China-CELAC Forum's five-year cooperation plan includes proposals for technical cooperation and financing.

When considered alongside other China's regional organizations, Chinese Academy of Social Sciences scholar, Xue Li, views the newly-established China-CELAC Forum as indicative of China's "diplomatic transformation," or the development of an increasingly prominent diplomatic presence in various regions of the world.

China also recently announced several new Latin America-focused credit lines and investment funds. In addition to the credit lines associated with the China-CELAC Forum, China's central bank announced this month that it will establish a $10 billion fund for investment in Latin American manufacturing. An additional $10 billion is being funneled to the BRICS-led New Development Bank.

3. *Many Chinese firms have improved their operations in Latin America, but Chinese economic engagement might still be affecting regional standards.*

Recent case study analysis suggests that Chinese companies have made considerable advances in community relations and adherence to local environmental and labor standards. They are, in certain cases, operating on par with or even better than other foreign firms in Latin America. Complaints about Chinese companies continue to surface, however. And the environmental standards of China's top lenders to Latin America – China Development Bank and China Ex-Im Bank – are still weaker than those of other international financial institutions.

There are also indications that some Latin American governments have intentionally weakened investment and other standards or disregarded existing regulations in order to attract Chinese and other investment, or to facilitate cross-Pacific trade. This is especially the case in sectors – e.g., mining, oil & natural gas, and agriculture – in which Chinese firms are quite active. Examples include recent changes to Peru's mining sector regulations and Ecuador's removal of local partner stipulations in exchange for dam financing.

In addition, China's ongoing and extensive financial support for certain governments in the region, such as Nicolás Maduro's in Venezuela, is thought to enable continued economic mismanagement and to facilitate corruption and standards erosion. China is committed to establishing a long-term presence in Venezuela, which has the largest proven oil reserves in the world. By our calculations, the country has received approximately US $50 billion in loans from Chinese banks since 2005. Many of these loans are repaid in oil.

Looking Ahead

China is and will continue to be an important economic partner for many countries in the region, even as economic growth slows on both sides of the Pacific. Latin America is a key destination as Beijing seeks to ensure domestic food and energy security. And LAC's commodities exporters largely depend on Chinese demand.

Latin America will also remain a critical market for an increasingly wide variety of Chinese goods, from cell phones and fabrics to high speed trains and electricity transmission infrastructure.

Whether China-Latin America relations are in fact "win-win" and "mutually beneficial," as China indicates, is debatable. Chinese trade is thought to have contributed considerably to regional economic growth in recent years. But Chinese economic engagement benefits some countries far more than others. Mexico, for example, has a considerable trade deficit with China. China's focus on Latin America's commodities has also resulted in export "primarization," or growing shares of primary commodities in certain countries' export baskets. As global commodities prices fall, South American nations in particular are feeling the effects of excessive dependence on the export of commodities.

Chinese investment could be helpful (even transformative) for some LAC industries/sectors (e.g., renewable energy or electricity transmission in Brazil). But "mutual benefit" will require LAC governments to negotiate effectively and maintain necessary environmental, labor, and other standards. Broader efforts to diversify China's economic engagement and to improve regional competitiveness would also promote a longer-term "win" for Latin America.

Mr. DUNCAN. I want to thank all the witnesses for their testimony. That was excellent and kind of a great segue into my line of questioning.

I will now recognize myself for 5 minutes in the first round.

So I spoke in my opening statement about John Kerry's words, that the end of the Monroe Doctrine was upon us. And we have kind of seen a U.S. disengagement in the region. It just doesn't rest with this President; it actually transcends a number of Presidents.

So do you believe—and I am asking all witnesses—do you believe the lack of U.S. leadership and engagement in Latin America and the Caribbean and Secretary Kerry's comment there, the Monroe Doctrine is over, has impacted China's objectives and actions in Latin America?

Dr. Ellis?

Mr. ELLIS. It is a wonderful and very important question.

Mr. DUNCAN. Is your microphone on there?

Mr. ELLIS. A wonderful and very important question, Mr. Chairman.

I have the opportunity to interact regularly with colleagues in China, and I remember at least three colleagues shortly after Secretary Kerry's speech before the OAS actually called me or emailed me saying, did he really mean it?

Clearly, China looks for signals, and I think that was an important signal that, at the very least, China should not decelerate its pursuit of economic and strategic objectives in the region.

And, certainly, while our Department of State has done some very credible and very good work and thinking on the topic, clearly, with some of the difficulties with respect to U.S. embassies and some of the lack of Presidential-level engagement on this topic, respectfully, I think Latin America has clearly perceived that lack. And, in that vacuum, I think, as well, when one takes a look at the relative lack of definitions for what the United States has to offer the region, that China's seemingly value-neutral, you know, "Take our money, we will help you develop," fills that vacuum.

Mr. DUNCAN. Yeah.

Dr. Dussel Peters?

Mr. DUSSEL PETERS. Yes. I would agree very strongly with you that we perceive on the one hand this lack of a U.S. commitment and interest in Latin America in general and particularly regarding this new triangular relationship, no?

This is why I proposed at the end that the United States should actively participate in these institutions that already exist in Latin America, such as CELAC, among others, but that the U.S. should also try to create new institutions and to create new knowledge in academic, public, and private institutions in the United States.

We have a lack of interest from the United States, a lack of active participation, and, as I stated in the beginning, a very clear long-term strategy from the perspective of the Chinese public sector.

Mr. DUNCAN. Okay.

Ms. Joseph-Harris, I am going to ask the question to you little bit differently. And let me first say that—a very impressive resume, and I look forward to reading some of your works.

So let me ask you the same question just kind of a different way. Do you think if the U.S. was engaged more and looking for trade opportunities and reaching out, spending more time focused on this hemisphere and working with our neighbors and friends here, do you think that would create less of an opportunity for China?

Ms. JOSEPH-HARRIS. Thank you very much, Chairman.

Firstly, what escapes us sometimes is that the U.S. does, in fact, have a fairly strong trade relationship with the Caribbean and Latin America. That is a historic relationship. However, the engagement appears to have weakened immediately after the events of 9/11. There was a dropping of the ball, as it were, as America, and rightly so, needed to redirect much of its interest to the Middle East. And that is the period in which China saw as a strategic opportunity. And there is where many of the inroads have been made diplomatically, economically, and culturally.

However, we have a very strong history of interoperability between our respective militaries, you know, and that is something that we should seize upon and consolidate. And one of the things that I had said in my original text is that without security and good governance there could be no chance of economic sustainability.

So we need to revisit that strong history of interoperability, continue to properly fortify the CBSI initiatives, and then build from there in terms of exploring areas that have been falling off in trade, like the CBSI, begin to explore those areas and see how we could improve.

But I am pretty hopeful that it can be done. We have a recent change in political administration in Guyana and Trinidad and Tobago recently, and those very countries had been instrumental in the early 2000s in bringing together a robust security architecture.

So we continue to look to the United States and our colleagues in the military and the security industries to invigorate those types of relationships.

Thank you, Chairman.

Mr. DUNCAN. Thank you.

Ms. Myers, do you think the lack of U.S. engagement opens a void? And do you think that China would not have this opportunity if the U.S. was more engaged?

Ms. MYERS. Absolutely. I believe the U.S. disengagement in the region has provided considerable space for China and other partners, economic partners, to engage quite a bit over the past few years.

But I think this also has to do with what many Chinese scholars are calling diplomatic transformation. And this is not a well-defined concept, but I think the general idea is the development of a diplomacy or a diplomatic presence that is consistent now with China's global growing role and the ''one road, one belt'' strategy, as described in this forum, as are new initiatives over the past couple of years, like the China-CELAC forum in Latin America.

So there is kind of an enhanced interest also in, basically during the Xi Jinping administration, in promoting a new form of diplomacy, more or less.

Mr. DUNCAN. All right.

My time is just about up. I just want to ask Dr. Dussel Peters, what do you think about the railroad between Peru and Brazil?

You know, China is investing this kind of money. You know, with the lack of any sort of highways and other ways other than the Amazon to move goods and services and people around, the railroad could be a game changer.

What are your thoughts about that?

Mr. DUSSEL PETERS. Look, I would say, in general, this proposal and this project goes hand-in-hand with what China has been proposing in the last 2 years under this heading, also, of the "New Silk Road," the "one belt, one road" strategy, which means focusing development on infrastructure, no? So there are a group of fundings. We have added up more than $150 billion U.S. dollars that China has been committing for infrastructure projects, and this project could be one of these.

By the way, you have to be careful also that not all the partners of this project have been informed of the project, no? Which means this project was launched in Brazil, and other countries such as Peru were also informed by the news, no? Usually you would think that you would work the other way around, which means you would work 2 years and then you inform about this publicly, no?

Mr. DUNCAN. Right.

Mr. DUSSEL PETERS. It is not the only project that has been launched this way. And there are a group of big projects all over Latin America that can change the geo-strategy in this new triangular relationship very profoundly, particularly the Canal of Nicaragua that is very close to the United States.

Mr. DUNCAN. Thank you very much. My time is up.

We were there in November last year, Congressman Yoho, Congressman Salmon, with Chairman Royce. And just knowing the geography and watching that, it is fascinating to me that they would do that. I look forward to talking more about that.

I recognize the ranking member for 5 minutes.

Mr. SIRES. Thank you.

Thank you for your comments.

Getting back to these projects, you know, you read about these projects—$100 billion, $50 billion. How realistic are some of these projects? I mean, this canal, how realistic is this, or is this just propaganda?

Ms. Myers, we will start with you. You are shaking your head. You don't think it——

Ms. MYERS. I have strong beliefs about the canal.

Well, since it was first discussed in 2013, there has been really no progress, either in terms of construction or in terms of finance, as far as we know. There is a considerable lack of transparency surrounding this entire project, so it is difficult to tell.

The general consensus is that, in order for this to proceed, it needs to be funded by a government, and specifically in this case China. But there is no clear evidence at this point that China is backing this project in particular. In fact, China has tried to distance itself from the Nicaragua Canal, unlike all of these other major infrastructure projects that it has proposed throughout the region. And these others are big, too, and extremely expensive.

So I don't see much progress in the coming years. We have seen the construction of an access road, a gravel road, some lights. There are many, many promises of additional milestones, but they tend to never come to pass.

Mr. SIRES. Dr. Dussel Peters?

Mr. DUSSEL PETERS. I agree that there has been little progress in this project in the last months, but I would take it very seriously, very seriously in terms that, A, it has not been disregarded by the Chinese public sector; B, the public sector and the central government in China have massive resources for this kind of project, as in the case of Brazil, as in other projects in Mexico and others, and I can imagine that this might be a concrete bargaining coin for the future for some kind of other negotiations, no?

Thank you.

Mr. SIRES. Dr. Ellis?

Mr. ELLIS. I think an important point which you raised by this is the fact that perhaps 80 percent of all of the projects that we commonly talk about do not ultimately happen, but those 20 percent and also the expectations raised by this are reshaping the region.

I concur that the Nicaragua Canal project is probably about 6 months behind schedule and is probably on the point of falling apart. We can mention other projects, from investment in Pampa de Pongo, the mine in Peru, Rio Blanco, others, the failed Dragon Mart project in Mexico, the Mexico City-Queretaro railroad. The list goes on and on.

And the fact is that not only do the Chinese have difficulty in engaging with the region, but, for that reason, many of the projects fall apart. However, the fact is that the projects that do go through—approximately $55 billion in investment to Venezuela, about $12 billion to Ecuador—reshapes and keeps alive those ALBA countries.

The net effect on trade relationships is we are moving toward what experts call the reprimatization of the region, which actually makes them much more vulnerable, the region much more vulnerable, as we see declining commodity demand right now.

We are seeing a shift in the institutional balance of the region. When we say, well, what keeps UNASUR alive, what keeps CELAC alive, and why are countries pulling away from the inter-American system, the OAS, one has to look at the impulse, the inspiration of being able to turn to Chinese markets even if some of those key projects are indeed in doubt.

Mr. SIRES. Thank you.

Ms. Joseph-Harris, I don't read about too many projects in the Caribbean from the Chinese. What are they doing in the Caribbean?

Ms. JOSEPH-HARRIS. Thank you so much, because I did have a list of very, very specific projects in the region, and I am glad I have the opportunity now to elaborate on it.

Just bear with me. Okay. Here we are.

In terms of the specific projects——

Mr. SIRES. Still working on it.

Ms. JOSEPH-HARRIS. I think I have it here. Yeah.

In relation to Jamaica, the Bahamas, Trinidad and Tobago, Grenada, and Barbados, I have made some very, very specific pointers identifying where these projects were.

In the case of Trinidad and Tobago, the Chinese have built a children's hospital. They have built a national arts performing center.

In the case of Jamaica, they have made huge investments in the sphere of what you will call "investment critical infrastructure hoteliering."

In the area of the Bahamas, they have also gone into critical infrastructure, port, and hoteliering.

In Grenada, they have invested considerably in what you will call cultural centers and so.

In Guyana, they have also invested in the bauxite industry, in terms of writing off at least nine major loans.

In Suriname, they have gone into mining.

And it is a long list. And what I am saying, essentially, is that some of these countries, we have to look at the strategic importance. Trinidad and Tobago is a provider of natural gas to the United States. In the case of Guyana, you have gold. In the case of Suriname, you also have gold. In Jamaica, you have bauxite. And this is a materializing of the Chinese quest to go after resources, raw materials, in anticipation of the global looming shortage that is around the bend.

In addition to which, there are ALBA members, members of the Bolivarian Alliance that are also CARICOM, Caribbean community members. And as China allies with many of these countries, it may be very inadvertently empowering the alliance, which is ideologically adverse to American and Western-style neoliberalism and institutions.

So one has to look at the Chinese asymmetric approaches, the way in which they model their diplomacy. They are trading with members of the Caribbean community who are members of the Bolivarian Alliance, empowering them, splitting allegiances, and thereby tilting the balance in terms of the U.S. influence within the region.

Another very interesting area is in what I would look at as the currency wars, asymmetric types of warfare. You may or may not be aware, Chairman, that recently, in July of this year, an agreement was signed with the Bahamian Government and the Chinese to go into arrangements with trading the renminbi. And the possibilities are that other members of the Caribbean community may be able to access trade through that form of currency as distinct from trading with the U.S.

So one has to look at the matrix of indirect relations—currency diplomacy, port diplomacy—and the very unique types of modeling that the Chinese are using that are by no means normal. And these are the areas in which the U.S. influence is gradually being eroded.

Thank you, Chairman.

Mr. SIRES. My time is up. Thank you very much.

Mr. DUNCAN. I thank the ranking member.

I will now turn to Chairman Salmon for 5 minutes.

Mr. SALMON. Thank you.

I would like to kind of follow along the same line of questioning as the chairman, Chairman Duncan, started, with U.S. involvement, U.S. presence in the region.

And I am going to turn to you, Dr. Ellis, first. I believe that Chairman Duncan is frustrated—I know we have had conversations—that, while the U.S. presence in the region seems to be not as strong as it could be, where there has been a vacuum—I think, Ms. Myers, you referenced that—and while China's influence seems to be growing in the region, my question is: If we could get a TPP agreement, would China's influence in the region grow, would the United States' influence in the region grow, or would it diminish on either side?

Mr. ELLIS. Thank you very much, Chairman Salmon. I think you raise an excellent question. And I, indeed, in my own writings, have been a strong advocate of a TPP, but certainly an effective and well-negotiated final TPP.

What I see is for both our Asian partners and our Latin American partners, the question is this emerging importance of the trans-Pacific. What are the rules that governs economic interactions? Will it be a Pacific in which the states which are larger and better able to coordinate their government and financial and commercial institutions can kick open the door, bring away intellectual property, impose their labor laws and workers on others? Or is it a rule-of-law Pacific environment in which there is respect for labor laws, in which there is respect for intellectual property, in which all states have the opportunity to reap the fruit of their hard work and good policies, whether Japan or China or otherwise?

I certainly am a strong advocate of a future TPP which remains open to China but one in which we have a prosperous Pacific, in which China and the other players play by the rules. And I believe that that creates a bigger pie for all parts of the Pacific community.

Mr. SALMON. Well, in some parts of the Western Hemisphere, there still are some serious governance and rule-of-law concerns, issues——

Mr. ELLIS. Yes.

Mr. SALMON [continuing]. Some corruption issues, human rights abuses, lack of environmental consciousness, and organized violence in some parts of the Western Hemisphere.

So is that political and economic climate in the region, is it going to hamper China's ability to be able to function effectively or navigate in the region? Or are they pretty adept at navigating with these types of relationships? Could they serve as a model for greater government accountability and respect for the rule of law for these countries, or does China perpetuate these problems?

Mr. ELLIS. An excellent question.

China is very careful not to impose its own concept of a model but very happy to allow others to draw from China the lessons that they will.

What concerns me is, in many ways, there is a new ideological struggle that I see of the 21st century, represented to some degree by the model of states such as the ALBA states, a very statist concept of how you negotiate with Asia, versus that which is represented by, for example, our partners, the Trans-Pacific Partnership, but, as well, the Alliance of the Pacific.

What concerns me in states like Nicaragua and Ecuador and others, to a certain extent Bolivia, et cetera, is that the opportunity to have Chinese money allows populist leaders to do direct relationships, which gets them away from accountability and oversight as previously imposed by institutions such as the Inter-American Development Bank, et cetera.

And, in many ways, the reason why China has loaned so much to Venezuela, over $55 billion, but has had very little success in the projects that they have pursued very hard in countries like Mexico and Colombia and elsewhere is that those countries have established laws and institutions and strong bureaucracies and are less willing to bend to the Chinese rules, whereas countries such as Venezuela have been more willing to do state-to-state deals.

And, at the end of the day, that disadvantages not only Western businesses but, I believe, disadvantages the rule of law in the region. It encourages corruption and bad governance. And, really, it prejudices the people of the region and their long-term democratic interests and development, I believe.

Mr. SALMON. I am going to paraphrase then. What I am hearing you saying is that if the United States isn't deeply engaged through activities like TPP, if we are not leaders in the region, then there is a vacuum that is filled by others.

Is that something others on the panel would agree with? That if we are not actively engaged in determining what the rules of the road are for engagement in the Western Hemisphere, if we are not the leader through things like TPP, then countries like China have greater authority to dictate those rules of the road? Is that—it looks like most of you agree with that.

The other question I wanted to ask is, with some of the economic woes that are happening in China domestically, is that going to impact their ability to be able to interact in the region, with the financial crisis that they have been going through?

Do you think, Ms. Myers, that is going to impact their ability to be able to complete the agenda?

Ms. MYERS. Certainly, we have already seen a pretty remarkable decrease in trade with Latin America, especially in South America, commodities trade over the past year, in particular, but also before that. Also, turbulence in Chinese markets and the Shanghai Stock Exchange and then the recent devaluation of the yuan has had effect on global markets, obviously, and then so also has affected Latin America quite considerably and, especially, again, commodities exporters—Chile, Peru, and others.

And so, in the short term, yes, there is a considerable effect on Latin America, and this is troubling to many.

In the medium to long term, I think—well, in the medium term, at least, we will see considerably more demand still for Chinese goods, for Chinese commodities—or, I am sorry, for Latin American commodities, in particular, and for Chinese goods in Latin America. These things aren't going to change immediately. Growth has slowed in trade, but it is still growing.

And China very much is looking not only to Latin America but to other regions for raw materials, of course, but also to help it facilitate its reform process. So many of these investments promote, for example, economic upgrading, which is a major element of reform, or the use of excess steel in China, and that is a major problem in the domestic Chinese economy.

So we will see more, absolutely.

Mr. DUNCAN. Thank you, Chairman.

We will now go down to Mr. Rohrbacher from California.

Mr. ROHRABACHER. Thank you very much.

When we are discussing China and its influences, this is not just a situation where the United States wants to dominate the world and we want to make sure that people are listening to rock and roll instead of Chinese instruments playing their style of music.

I just note that in China there has been no political reform whatsoever. Although we had a promise that if we increased our economic ties to China, increased our investment, increased our involvement, that there would be a liberalization of their system. And there is no opposition party, opposition press. There are no people who are permitted to openly organize and criticize the government.

China has also, at the same time that it has no political reform, has become ever more aggressive in its many territorial claims, territorial claims which we have ignored for a long time, but now they seem to be reemerging. Plus, you have military action taken by China over dubious claims in the South China Sea.

So as we are discussing the issue of China's influence, it is not just another country versus our country as our influence. It is whether or not this totalitarian power will be expanding its area of influence, but in some ways control.

And let me also note this. Years ago there was—I first noted this when—and the Chinese targets and how they handle it economically—when the Panama Canal, as it exists today, a Chinese company was able to buy—Hutchison Whampoa was able to buy terminals on both sides of the canal, thus putting the Panama Canal in a position of being dominated by this Chinese-owned company, and how that company received that contract after the actual Panamanian Government had been notified, an American company, that they had won the contract, and they were there to accept the contract. In the middle of the conversation, a phone call comes in. And I think it was the Vice President had to leave the office. And when he came back, he said: Oh, there was a mistake made. The contract went to somebody else.

And the question, what I am leading into is, it was always my belief that somebody had been paid off. In the United States, we put our people in jail if they make bribes to foreign leaders. Is there any such rule of thumb for the way the Chinese companies deal with these Third World countries that we are talking about and developing countries?

Mr. ELLIS. Well, certainly China does have rules. However, its understanding of how those rules restrain it and the degree to which it enforces those rules, especially with respect to companies overseas, is a gray area. Indeed, many fear that one of the sources of a reduction in Chinese foreign overseas investment may be that the crackdown on SOE heads in China itself may make China's leaders reluctant to pursue deals which would lead to their personal enrichment in places in Latin America.

77

But certainly the deeper question that you raise is a very important one, and that is that to the extent that you do not have an analog of the Foreign Corrupt Practices Act, those type of deals increase corruption in the region at two levels.

Mr. ROHRABACHER. When you come from a society that doesn't have a rule of law, doesn't have an independent judiciary, doesn't have stated rights in terms of people's relationship with legal procedures and who owns what property, et cetera, you would expect that in that country there would be some major problems in dealing with the citizens and companies from that country.

Let me ask you this about those companies that are dealing with these nations that we are talking about. Many of the companies in China that are making profits, et cetera, are actually companies that are owned by the People's Liberation Army. Are any of the companies that you are talking about owned by the People's Liberation Army?

Mr. ELLIS. Probably one of the best examples that comes up—and of course ownership is a difficult concept. We talked about the Nicaragua Canal. And when we take a look at the mysterious Mr. Wang Jing, although he is basically a defense contractor in the Chinese parlance, the offices that he has in the region and Hong Kong are filled with, you know, patriotic paraphernalia, however, when one actually looks at his primary company, a telecommunications company called Xinwei, which is involved in building a system-of-systems type of infrastructure for the PLA, the way that he got to be a very young 47-something-year-old billionaire is because he made a leveraged buyout to this company and then miraculously that company began getting billions of dollars of contracts from the PLA.

And so certainly aside from Hutchison and your very good point about Hutchison's relation—and Hutchison, of course, was just recently bought by a mainland Chinese company—but I think one of the things that worries me about Wang Jing is the fact that those ties through Xinwei indicate that certainly there are certainly interests. If there are commercial interests, there are interests behind those interests. And I think, you know, that that needs to be a concern as we look at the nature of the relationship in the future.

Mr. ROHRABACHER. Anybody on the People's Liberation Army?

Ms. MYERS. I just wanted to add that Wang Jing's company, Xinwei, just declared bankruptcy. So it kind of bodes poorly, I think, for the canal operation as well, considering that he is funding much of the first sort of elements of that.

Mr. DUSSEL PETERS. In our experience, the public sector in China is omnipresent in qualitative terms. It is not sufficient to go very concretely regarding one public institution, but you have the central government, you have cities, you have municipalities, and the mixture of these governments, the public sector.

To have an idea, more than 86 percent of Chinese FDI, according to the work we have been doing from 2000 to 2013, has been pursued 86 percent by the Chinese public sector. So there is an omnipresent public sector participating in FDI.

And I would briefly relate to the question that was posed regarding TPP by the chairman and Mr. Salmon. I think TPP is not sufficient as a Latin American strategy. TPP is dividing Latin America, a group of Latin American countries are not geographically related to the Pacific. And I would highlight how important it would be to modernize, to rediscuss, for example, a topic such as NAFTA, which has been completely left aside. I would very strongly propose to upgrade, to modernize——

Mr. DUNCAN. In the essence of time, I am going to need you to wrap up. Try to respect the other members' time. I know Ms. Joseph-Harris wants to respond.

If you could do it briefly. This gentleman has somewhere else to go and I want to try to get to him. So, Ms. Joseph-Harris, if you will just respond briefly.

Ms. JOSEPH-HARRIS. Thank you. I will get to the crux of it.

What we are looking at, Chairman, is that we are in an ideological war. The member is quite correct, it is ideological. And I would even go so far as to say that the whole idea, the whole notion of a China-U.S. dynamic is ideologically based. And I would cite what I mean by it.

America's ideological apparatus, represented by its globally dispersed network of central banks, international monetary system, multilateral corporations, vis—vis a Chinese facade, where you have no democracy, no rule of law, that brings us in what you call a juxtaposition, it is an ideological face-off.

This is what we are looking at, and that whatever we are looking at ties back to ideas and ideology. And what makes the Caribbean, in particular, vulnerable is the fact that we lack that strong ideological base, save and except for the institutional formidability of the OAS, which is the only strong and true multilateral forum. And that is where we need to look at the institution within the Americas as a countervailing effect against China.

Thank you, Chairman.

Mr. DUNCAN. Great points.

Mr. Yoho.

Mr. YOHO. Mr. Chairman, I appreciate it.

I appreciate you all being here today.

And it is disheartening to see that we are losing our influence with our closest allies, our closest countries, and that China is kicking our rear end again.

And I wanted to ask you, before I ask any questions, Dr. Dussel Peters, I am glad to hear you say that the TPP really wouldn't help the area. It would be us negotiating a strong trade agreement with all of Latin America. And you would agree with that?

Mr. DUSSEL PETERS. Yes, very strongly.

Mr. YOHO. Okay.

And then the other thing is what I see as a stale relationship, it is like a relationship between people, the United States and Latin America, it has become stale. We need to revitalize that. And from what I have heard from you, it is from a lack of engagement. And I know after 9/11 there was a cause for that, but we need to move on. And we need to reinvest in our closest allies before other people.

And I think we need to restate the Monroe Doctrine. I think that is something that we need to stand for what the Western Hemisphere stands for. Because what we have seen over the course of the last 20 years is a slip or a slide into socialism. They are lining up with Iran. They are lining up with Russia and China. And we are losing that influence.

And what I wanted to ask you is, why is that, and what has caused that? Is it because America, our country, meddles too much in telling other countries how to live, the kind of rule of law they should have, and our ideologies? And I know China doesn't do that as much. They kind of just go with the flow and invest in the infrastructures.

What are your thoughts on that, Dr. Ellis? Are we meddling too much in telling people how to live?

Mr. ELLIS. I think that to some degree the right kind of meddling is useful. One of the dilemmas that China finds itself in right now, for example, with the change in government in Guyana, the new, very effective government of Dr. David Granger, China suddenly finds that the dirty deals that it makes with one government, when it is replaced by another government, it now finds problems. It faces the same dilemma——

Mr. YOHO. I am glad they find that.

Mr. ELLIS. But I think also, with all respect, one of the things that I believe that we need more of—and it is ironic because it is a point that is made I think very effectively in the most recent defense and diplomacy review document that the State Department has put out—is value-based leadership.

In my respective judgment, what we have done—what we have not done sufficiently is explain why the U.S. concept of rule of law and free markets in democracy will bring broad-based development and why it is the best deal, why going with the easy deal with the Chinese money does not bring sustainable development, why going with particularistic negotiations between a leader and a Chinese company is not the best way to bring value added in the company involved. And I don't think that we do that effectively enough in explaining our case to the region.

Mr. YOHO. And I am glad you brought that up because what I have seen in other countries, especially in Africa and some of the other countries, China puts money into there, but then they suck the resources off and they leave. You are not getting a Chinese company. You are getting the Chinese government, their military, their secret service, and all that in one. It is not a Chinese company. I mean, it is a facade. We have seen that over and over again and we know that for a fact.

But I have to give them credit. They are making headway. They go in there and they get the trace minerals, the rare earth minerals, and they are smart at doing that. And we need to tighten up our strategy and our foreign policy.

Let me ask you, does the OAS, are they courting the Chinese? Are they shunning us, Ms. Joseph-Harris?

Ms. JOSEPH-HARRIS. Member Yoho, I really, really welcome this part of the discussion. I would like to tag onto what my colleagues said.

Mr. YOHO. Yeah, sure. You have got a minute and 18 seconds.

Ms. JOSEPH-HARRIS. We do, in fact, have a very robust inter-American institutional system under the OAS, and it is very open, sort of poised, positioned to do exactly that, sell the inter-American ideal to the community. And I think there is where we probably dropped the ball and we need to focus there on rebuilding that past. Thank you.

Mr. YOHO. Ms. Myers, do you have anything you want to add into that? Did I catch you off guard?

Ms. MYERS. Not on the OAS. But I would say that, I mean, at the very least, there was a Pew study, a Pew Research study that was done a couple of years ago on perceptions of China and the U.S. In Latin America. And it was very clear that the perceptions of the U.S. are still extremely strong. China is rising in certain respects. But we have a very strong relationship with Latin America and there is much to build on in that respect.

But, yes, in terms of finance, no-conditions finance is very appealing to many countries in the region. And for that reason, not only in terms of investment, but also in finance, there have been cases when Chinese companies and banks have won out over American companies and banks, and that is problematic.

Mr. YOHO. I appreciate everybody's answers.

Mr. Chairman, thank you for the opportunity.

Mr. DUNCAN. I want to thank the gentleman for staying around. I know you have got other places to be.

We will go to Mr. Smith from New Jersey.

Mr. SMITH. Chairman Duncan, thank you very much for the hearing, as well as for my good friend Matt Salmon, and, of course, Albio Sires. This is a very important subject, and I thank you for bringing some light and scrutiny to it.

A similar type of Chinese hegemony is actually occurring in Africa as well. I chair the Africa Committee. And I am very concerned, you know, sometimes, what is China's interest in Latin America, we also have to ask what is Latin America's interest in China? Increasingly for despotic regimes in places like Sudan, it is Bashir who greatly cherishes his relationship with Beijing. And, of course, Evo Morales and so many others, the FMLN in El Salvador, increasingly.

My first trip to Latin America was three times during the FMLN wars and saw upfront and close the terrible devastation. But who was providing those funds? It was all coming from the Soviet Union, usually by way of Cuba, and violence was being used for political means.

Now China is stepping into that void with the demise of the Soviet Union, and they are doing it all over the world. The bad governance model, as you know, is being very aggressively promoted.

I was in Bolivia twice in the last couple of years working on behalf of an American who was being held captive in Palmasola prison. Went to the prison. No charges were brought against him. Eighteen months in that hellhole. And Evo Morales and his government, and I while there became even more sensitized to it, just loved Tehran and just loved China because it is a source of legitimacy, for money, and trade.

So my concerns are, you know, we will have Xi Jinping coming to the United States and visiting with President Obama in just a few weeks, very, very shortly. I am doing a hearing before he comes on China's race to the bottom with North Korea on human rights abuses. They have gotten far worse. Name the issue, trafficking, torture, the crackdown on religious belief. And then you see that they are having additional and enhanced influence in the Caribbean, as well as in the rest of Central and South America. A very, very disturbing trend because dictatorships, whether it be in Venezuela or elsewhere, thrive on that kind of cooperation with a dictatorship like China.

So my first question or big question is, what is Latin America's interest? Why are these, these guerilla movements now turned, you know, whether it be FMLN or the FSLN in Nicaragua, finding such a friend in Beijing? Twelve countries in Central and South America and the Caribbean still support the Republic of China on Taiwan. Is there pressure being put on them to sever those ties or downgrade that recognition?

And, again, when it comes to providing arms, from AK-47s to everything else, when it comes to using the Internet to surveil dissidents and people who espouse real democracy, what is China's influence there? Because they have literally written the book on how to find good people, dissidents and others, track them down, and throw them into prison.

Mr. ELLIS. I think they are very good questions. China's interest, in my judgment—I am sorry, Latin America's interest—ranges from the legitimate and the commercial to the less legitimate. I think it is reasonable for many Latin American businessmen and leaders to see opportunities in Chinese markets, to see opportunities in attracting Chinese investment, to see new possibilities for funding sources.

Not all of those interests are illegitimate. However, it is a spectrum. Because as we move into other types of things, the opportunity of a Hugo Chavez and now Nicolas Maduro to be able to escape good financial oversight and democratic institutions and things like that because he can get the quick Chinese loan or now the $10 billion in new Chinese loans in the runup to the December 6 congressional elections in Venezuela.

And it goes into the personal as well. One takes a look at one of the sons of Daniel Ortega, Laureno Ortega, who was instrumental in putting together the Nicaragua Canal deal, as well as the telecom financing deal in Nicaragua with Xinwei.

And the fact is that the Chinese deal, in part because of the lack of oversight, provide both personal enrichment opportunities, as well as opportunities for leaders who don't want to have to adhere to the types of values that the United States is promoting, democracy, labor rights, free markets, transparency, to be able to get away from that.

But only get away from that for a time because ultimately it leads to a greater collapse, because of the economic contradictions, because of the poor governance. But when that collapse comes, it prejudices us because it is we in this hemisphere who are geographically, physically, economically, and by ties of family related to the hemisphere, whereas the consequences are much more indirect in terms of what happens when those deals go bad for China.

Mr. SMITH. I yield back my time.

Mr. DUNCAN. I thank the gentleman from New Jersey.

We will go to Mr. Chabot from Ohio.

Mr. CHABOT. Thank you very much, Mr. Chairman.

I will ask probably just one question here unless I have a follow-up. And I will address it to the whole panel to the extent you would like to answer it.

My question is in regards to China's objectives with respect to Taiwan and Tibet. In your opinion, is China strengthening its diplomatic relations with countries in the Western Hemisphere at least partly in an effort to isolate Taiwan and to some degree Tibet or a free Tibet some day? If yes, how successful have they been so far? And specifically what are the benefits that China offers to Latin American countries in exchange for their support in this effort to isolate especially Taiwan, but also to some degree Tibet? Whoever wants to take it first.

Ms. Joseph-Harris.

Ms. JOSEPH-HARRIS. Member Chabot, thank you very much. In the case of the Caribbean, it has been a rather interesting scenario. Within the CARICOM community, which is a 15-member coalition, we have a situation where there is an absence of what is called an Asian policy. And the Chinese have been very, very successful in penetrating that absence of policy by literally purchasing diplomatic relations in terms of inducing countries to split their allegiance and remove their relationship with Taiwan in favor of Beijing.

And the inducements have been large sums of money, donations, and cash. Less than diplomatic, one would say, but they have been extremely successful in it. So that, currently, there are, I would say, there are still four countries out of CARICOM left, and the Chinese are very aggressive in terms of getting them to withdraw that allegiance with Taiwan. So I would say that they have been very good at it thus far.

Mr. CHABOT. Thank you very much.

Yes, Dr. Peters.

Mr. DUSSEL PETERS. We have been working in the last years on the Central American countries and their relationship with China, and it has been very interesting how as a result of the improvement in the relationship between Taiwan and China, China has been extremely pragmatic regarding the issue of this diplomatic relationship and recognition, which means that China has been able to accept delegations from countries without a diplomatic relationship. They have been doing turnkey investments, trade, and a big group and an interesting dialogue, political dialogue also.

And I would tell you finally that in the region China has also increasingly stated that while it has offered a group of projects to Costa Rica who broke these relationships in the region, this will not happen again in the region. Also, again, this pragmatism even in the diplomatic arena is very important.

Mr. CHABOT. Thank you.

Dr. Ellis.

Mr. ELLIS. Yes. As you know, in 2008, then newly elected Taiwanese President Ma Ying-jeou formed an informal agreement with then Chinese President Hu Jintao to basically suspend this politics of the checkbook.

What has happened in general is that they have honored that relationship. But I also look toward the importance of the future. In other words, in that time since 2008, just about every Central

American and Caribbean president who has recognized Taiwan has expressed an interest in changing. We saw it with President Lugo, then president of Paraguay. We saw it with President Funes in El Salvador. We saw it with President Zelaya and later President Lobo in Honduras. We saw it with President Martinelli in Panama, et cetera, et cetera.

The Chinese have said no. But the way I look at it is that they have prioritized the resolution of their dispute between brothers over any short-term gains that they could get from Central America and the Caribbean. In that sense, I think it has been a lesson for where their priorities actually lie.

But what concerns me about that is that if that truce ever breaks down, it is very clear that China has been advancing its commercial engagement offices of CPIET, et cetera, so that if China decided to start accepting that interest in changing, very, very rapidly Taiwan would find itself without diplomatic recognition and in a grave situation diplomatically in the region.

Ms. CHABOT. Thank you, Doctor.

Ms. Myers, I have a little time left.

Ms. MYERS. Sure, just very briefly. I mean, there is a possibility that Tsai Ing-wen, the new candidate who is part of the DPP party, could win the next election. And, of course, she and her party are more supportive of Taiwanese independence than the KMT.

If that were the case, then we could see a sort of reemergence, there has been a diplomatic truce so far, but we could see a lot more competition between China and Taiwan in the region, especially in Central America and the Caribbean. I am not sure how that would play out, but there is a good possibility there.

And then just on the Dalai Lama, you see both sort of direct opposition to Dalai Lama visits, for example, and indirect. For example, you have a Confucius Institute in your university and you are receiving a lot of funding from China for that Confucius Institute, are you going to invite the Dalai Lama even though you might want to? Maybe not, because it certainly risks complete removal of all of that funding.

So you see certainly that sort of influence happening very, very indirect, very sort of under the table. But it is happening.

Mr. CHABOT. Thank you very much.

Thank you, Mr. Chairman.

Mr. DUNCAN. I want to thank the gentleman from Ohio. Great questions.

The Chair will now go to Mr. Sires from New Jersey for I think the final round of questions here.

Mr. SIRES. I have two observations. One of the observations that I have is that one of the reasons that our two regions are so tied together is the fact that this is a region where they have had many revolutions and the only country that really has opened their doors to all those people over the years has been this country. So it has developed an umbilical cord type of relationship that I think for China is going to be very difficult to break. I don't know if you agree with that or not.

And the other observation that I have is the OAS, Ms. Joseph-Harris, I disagree with you. I think it is completely ineffective. I think it is an organization that doesn't speak up enough on the abuses in this region. And if you are there to represent these countries, you are just too influenced by some of these countries not to speak up on the abuses that are going on. I mean, I haven't seen the OAS talk about Venezuela and the abuses of Venezuela at all. So when you tell me that you have an institution that could be a vehicle, I am sorry, I really don't see it as a vehicle. Not to mention the abuses in China, but, you know.

Ms. JOSEPH-HARRIS. I agree with you on the ineffectiveness of the OAS. I don't want to be misunderstood. But I am saying that there is an institutional framework. It needs to be empowered. It needs to be made effective. I am familiar with the framework because years ago I have been part of experts teams. But I am agreeing with you that a lot needs to be done in order to empower the OAS so that it can be effective. Thank you.

Mr. DUSSEL PETERS. I believe that, in fact, CELAC has been very successful in this dialogue with China. And I believe it would be very relevant for the United States to participate in CELAC. For whatever reason, OAS has not been active in this area.

Mr. ELLIS. Mr. Sires, I think you raise a very, very important question. Thank you for the opportunity.

To me, I agree with you that the OAS has deep, deep difficulties. When I look at this from a strategic perspective, though, I ask myself, is it in the interest of the United States to try to empower a debilitated institution or to let it die or be ineffective.

And when I look at the alternatives, it worries me. For example, China chose to engage with CELAC, which excludes the United States. Other states in the region, one could say Brazil, have interests in the empowerment of UNASUR to fight the region's interests as opposed to the OAS.

But if the OAS remained ineffective, we, in my judgment, do not have an effective vehicle. China was an observer member of the OAS since 2004, but they chose to work through CELAC. Our Colombian friends came asking for help from the OAS to resolve. To me, if we allow the OAS to be ineffective, and that goes down to leadership on our part, then we prejudice ourselves respectively strategically in the hemisphere. That is my respectful opinion.

Mr. SIRES. Ms. Myers, what do you think?

Ms. MYERS. We are hosting a meeting with the OAS today, and they have done a fantastic job of helping us out.

But, no, I mean, I would actually agree with Enrique that U.S. participation in some form in CELAC—I mean, it was the brain child of Hugo Chavez and so it almost intentionally did not include the U.S. and Canada. But I think at least in the initial observer capacity, whereby, you know, facilitating in some form some of the technical cooperation that has been proposed could be a good thing.

The OAS, obviously there is much to do there to improve its function. But I agree that it is also a useful organization to the extent that it can be more effective in the region.

Mr. SIRES. Mr. Chairman, thank you very much.

And thank you very much.

Mr. DUNCAN. I want to take this opportunity to thank the witnesses. I thought this was an excellent discussion. I don't know that we have solved any problems, but I don't know if that was the goal. But I learned a lot. And I think this dialogue about U.S. engagement and opportunities to allow others to get a foothold in our hemisphere is so critical.

And so I want to thank you. And I look forward to continuing this dialogue. I look forward to reading some of your material as well.

So pursuant to Rule 7, the members of the subcommittee will be permitted to submit written statements to be included in the official hearing record.

Without objection, the hearing record will remain open for 5 business days to allow statements, questions, and extraneous materials for the record, subject to the length limitation of the rules.

There being no further business for the committee, we will stand adjourned. Thanks so much.

[Whereupon, at 3:40 p.m., the subcommittees were adjourned.]

APPENDIX

Material Submitted for the Record

JOINT SUBCOMMITTEE HEARING NOTICE
COMMITTEE ON FOREIGN AFFAIRS
U.S. HOUSE OF REPRESENTATIVES
WASHINGTON, DC 20515-6128

Subcommittee on the Western Hemisphere
Jeff Duncan (R-SC), Chairman

Subcommittee on Asia and the Pacific
Matt Salmon (R-AZ), Chairman

TO: **MEMBERS OF THE COMMITTEE ON FOREIGN AFFAIRS**

You are respectfully requested to attend an OPEN hearing of the Committee on Foreign Affairs, to be held jointly by the Subcommittee on the Western Hemisphere and the Subcommittee on Asia and the Pacific in Room 2172 of the Rayburn House Office Building (and available live on the Committee website at http://www.ForeignAffairs.house.gov):

DATE: Thursday, September 10, 2015

TIME: 2:00 p.m.

SUBJECT: China's Advance in Latin America and the Caribbean

WITNESSES: Evan Ellis, Ph.D.
Author
China on the Ground in Latin America

Enrique Dussel Peters, Ph.D.
Director
Center for Chinese-Mexican Studies
School of Economics
National Autonomous University of Mexico

Ms. Serena Joseph-Harris
Chief Executive Officer
Sirius International (Caribbean) Defense Contractors Ltd.
(*Former High Commissioner of the Republic of Trinidad and Tobago*)

Ms. Margaret Myers
Program Director
China and Latin America
Inter-American Dialogue

By Direction of the Chairman

The Committee on Foreign Affairs seeks to make its facilities accessible to persons with disabilities. If you are in need of special accommodations, please call 202/225-5021 at least four business days in advance of the event, whenever practicable. Questions with regard to special accommodations in general (including availability of Committee materials in alternative formats and assistive listening devices) may be directed to the Committee.

COMMITTEE ON FOREIGN AFFAIRS

MINUTES OF SUBCOMMITTEE ON _____ *The Western Hemisphere and Asia and the Pacific* _____ HEARING

Day __*Thursday*__ Date __*September 10, 2015*__ Room _____ 2172 _____

Starting Time __*2:22 p.m.*__ Ending Time __*3:40 p.m.*__

Recesses _____ (____ to ____) (____ to ____) (____ to ____) (____ to ____) (____ to ____) (____ to ____)

Presiding Member(s)

Chairman Jeff Duncan

Check all of the following that apply:

Open Session ☑   Electronically Recorded (taped) ☑
Executive (closed) Session ☐   Stenographic Record ☑
Televised ☐

TITLE OF HEARING:

"*China's Advance in Latin America and the Caribbean*"

SUBCOMMITTEE MEMBERS PRESENT:

Reps. Duncan, Sires, Salmon, Rohrbacher, Smith, Chabot, Yoho

NON-SUBCOMMITTEE MEMBERS PRESENT: *(Mark with an * if they are not members of full committee.)*

HEARING WITNESSES: Same as meeting notice attached? Yes ☑ No ☐
(If "no", please list below and include title, agency, department, or organization.)

STATEMENTS FOR THE RECORD: *(List any statements submitted for the record.)*

Rep. Christopher Smith

TIME SCHEDULED TO RECONVENE _____
or
TIME ADJOURNED __*3:40 p.m.*__

Subcommittee Staff Director

Rep. Chris Smith
Western Hemisphere/A&P Subcommittees
"China's Advance in Latin America & the Caribbean"
September 10, 2015

I would like to thank our witnesses for testifying at today's hearing, and to thank Chairmen Duncan and Salmon, as well as Ranking Members Sires and Sherman, for convening today's hearing.

In addition to asking "What is China's interest in Latin America," we should ask "What is Latin America's interest in China?"

For the governments of Latin America are not passive actors. Rather, many are highly ideological ones whose stated values diverge from our ideals and principles.

As was very clear to me during two trips I took to Bolivia seeking to free an American, Jacob Ostreicher, who had been unjustly imprisoned, there is a strong anti-American rhetorical undercurrent in Latin America, one which expresses itself in policy terms by seeking allies who, ultimately, are not friends of the United States. In the case of Bolivia, the tilt to Communist China was very obvious and apparent, as was an embrace of the radical Shiite Islamist regime in Tehran.

We ignore ideology at our own peril. There is a self-styled Bolivarian movement in Latin America, known by its Spanish-language acronym ALBA, translated variously in English as the Bolivarian Alternative to the Americas or the Bolivarian Alliance for the People of Our America. Venezuela and Cuba are its founding members, but since 2004 the ALBA movement has been joined by left-wing governments in Bolivia, Nicaragua, and Ecuador, as well as countries in the Caribbean. El Salvador, though not yet formally a member, is drifting into the ALBA orbit under the left-wing government of the FMLN, a former guerilla movement.

There also was a movement of New Left forces, which grew out of the São Paulo Forum, or Foro de São Paulo, held in Brazil in 1990. In the wake of the Fall of the Berlin Wall, various Left Wing movements gathered to renounce armed revolution as the path to power, embracing instead democratic mechanisms as a vehicle for obtaining power. Once in place, however, many of these regimes utilize propaganda, the distribution of economic spoils and anti-Americanism to retain power. While Venezuela might be the most extreme example of such a rise to power, we see similar paths to power taken by Workers Party in Brazil and the Kirchner-faction Peronists in Argentina.

This is important background to keep in mind as we listen to today's speakers, and consider Latin America's outreach to China and vice versa. It is folly to ignore the power of ideology, and how that may motivate the very real challenge to American economic leadership posed, for example, by the emergence of the BRICS nations centered around Brazil and China. Such a challenge is evident also in efforts at partnership by China and Nicaragua, aimed at building a canal to rival the Panama Canal.

To ignore this trend is folly, as is a policy that seeks to embrace hostile regimes and ignore or undermine friends. This Administration in particular has made missteps in reaching out to Venezuela and Cuba without first seeing a reciprocal movement away from anti-Americanism and in respect for the human rights of the Venezuelan and Cuban people.

Finally, this need to distinguish between friends and enemies is also pertinent when considering that not only China plays a role in the region, but so too does Taiwan. Some 12 countries in Latin America and the Caribbean continue to recognize the government of the Republic of China on Taiwan.

In particular, I would focus on two that do: Nicaragua and El Salvador. Both these countries have left-wing governments led by former communist guerillas. Communist China has courted Nicaragua in particular, dangling dreams of a canal. Unlike China, Taiwan does not seek rivalry with the United States, and indeed, by retaining diplomatic relations with El Salvador and Nicaragua, is protecting our rear flank. As these governments consider dalliances with China, we would be wise to cultivate our friendship with Taiwan, in addition to cultivating friendship with countries such as Colombia which reject the siren song of anti-American ideology.

Thank you.